D1649428

FRENCH VOCABULARY TOOLKIT

CONTENTS

	Introduction	2
1	Self, family & friends	6
2	Local area & weather	10
3	School life	14
4	Education, careers & future plans	18
5	Travel & transport	22
6	Finding the way	26
7	Holidays, tourism & tourist information	28
8	Accommodation	32
9	People & places	36
10	Services (bank, post office, telephone, lost property)	40
11	Illness, accidents & injuries	44
12	House & home	48
13	Life at home	52
14	Special occasions	56
15	Food & drink	60
16	Eating out	64
17	Healthy living	68
18	The world of work	70
19	Leisure activities	74
20	Media (cinema, television, theatre)	78
21	People & personalities	82
22	Meeting people	86
23	Shopping	90
24	Fashion & clothes	94
25	Current affairs & social issues	98
26	Miscellaneous vocabulary	102
	Answers	104

Welcome to the French Vocabulary Toolkit!

The aim of this book is to help you to learn the vocabulary which you will need to do well in the GCSE examination in French. The vocabulary listed in the book is based on the word lists in the specifications of the Edexcel awarding body and will be particularly useful if you are preparing for an Edexcel examination.

You will not be allowed to use a dictionary in your examinations, so it is important that you have a good knowledge of vocabulary to back you up. The more words you know, the easier you will find it to do the questions well. Just as you can't build a house without bricks, you can't write in French without the words to put into the sentences.

Structure of the book

This book is arranged in topics, which cover the topics required by the Specifications common to all the awarding bodies. The titles are given at the beginning of each section. In addition, each section uses colour to show the gender of the nouns. Masculine nouns are printed in blue (un/le); feminine nouns are printed in red (une/la). Verbs are printed in green. All other types of word are printed in black. (There is some evidence to show that colour coding helps one remember which gender group a word belongs to by picturing the colour groups on the page.) An asterisk (*) denotes vocabulary which only appears at Higher level.

The activities

After the list of words in each topic, there are a number of activities which will help you check whether you have learned the words. You should only do these activities when you have finished learning the vocabulary.

It would be possible to do the activities by writing the answers into the book, but it would be much better to write your answers onto a separate piece of paper. You could then do the activities several times – the more often you use the words the better they will become fixed in your memory. You will also be able to revise as the exam approaches.

Maybe you have bought the book a few weeks before the examination! In this case, do the exercises first. This will help you to find out which words you know and which ones you need to learn.

You will find the answers to the activities at the back of the book. Only look at the answers once you have done the exercises! Then you will find out which words you really have learnt. Don't look first! It won't help you to learn the words; it will only make you think that you know more than you really do.

You may have some answers which are different from the ones provided. This could well be the case. Don't automatically assume that you are wrong. Check with your teacher to see if your answer is also possible. (Maybe you could write to us at Collins and we could include your answers in a future edition!)

Vocabulary learning

Vocabulary learning is an essential part of learning a foreign language and there are no short cuts. You have to build up your vocabulary by learning it slowly and gradually. Good linguists have a large vocabulary.

If you manage to learn ten words every day from Monday to Friday and use the weekend to revise them, you will learn 50 words a week. If you learn 50 words a week, you will learn 200 words in a month. 200 words every month means that you learn 2400 in a year. And 2400 words is more than enough for GCSE!

People learn vocabulary in different ways. You need to find the way which is best for you and use it regularly. In the next section we give you some tips on how to learn vocabulary. Try some of them out and you may find that learning vocabulary is more fun than you thought it was.

Amuse-toi bien!

Tips on vocabulary learning

1 Keep this book with you all the time. Use it when you have a spare moment. Every little helps! Test yourself regularly. Tick the words you really do know and concentrate on the ones you need to learn.

2   Use this book often: while you are waiting for the bus; on the bus; when you have a few minutes to spare at home.

3   Write out the words which you are finding difficult to learn. Write them slowly and carefully. Write them four or five times each.

4   Keep a separate notebook for words which you come across which are not in this book. Use this notebook in the same way: go through it regularly, so that you learn these words too. The more words you know, the easier you will find it to do the tests in the examination.

5   Make a set of vocabulary cards. Write the English word on one side of the card and the French word on the other. Go through the cards, testing yourself on the words. Put the words you know to one side. If you don't know a word, put it at the bottom of the pack, so that it comes up again until you really do know it.

6   Get your parents, a relation or a friend to test you on the words you have to learn. It doesn't matter if they don't speak French. If they aren't sure if you got the word right, get them to ask you to spell it.

7   Write down the words on little notes and put them around the house in places where you will see them regularly, e.g. by the television; in the bathroom; on the stairs; by the computer; by your bed; on the fridge. Tell your parents this is a vital part of your learning for GCSE!

8   Use your vocabulary cards in the same way. Put one by the front door. Every time you come in or go out, look at the English word, say the foreign word, then turn the card over to see if you got it right. When you are sure you know the word, change the card for another one.

9   Say the words out loud when you are learning them. It helps you to remember them.

10 Make a cassette to help you learn the words. Write down a list of the English words and the French words. Speak the English words out loud one by one onto the cassette. After each English word, say the French word to yourself twice, without speaking out loud. This leaves a gap on the tape. When you have finished, play the tape and try to say the foreign word in the gap on the tape. When you can do this quickly for all the words, you will have learnt them. You can use the tape on your walkman.

11 If you are having difficulties remembering a word, ask a friend (or a teacher) to ask you what it is every time they pass you in the corridor. Make it into a kind of joke. You'll soon learn it then!

12 And don't forget to try and learn a small number of words each day. Remember: 10 a day = 50 a week = 200 a month = 2400 a year.

Success at GCSE!

A note to parents

You can help your son or daughter by supporting them in their vocabulary learning. Even if you don't speak French, you can probably tell whether they know the word or not. If you are not sure, ask your son or daughter to spell it.

Allow your child to put some of the vocabulary learning tips into practice. It may mean having a lot of notes around your home and will make dusting difficult for a while - but you will be pleased when your child passes GCSE!

Take an interest in their vocabulary-learning and encourage them to do it. Try to have a regular time each day (e.g. after a meal) when you listen to the words they have learnt. Most children need a structure to help them learn. You can provide that.

un adulte	adult
l'âge	age
un agent de police	police officer
un ami	friend
un an	year
un animal (pl: animaux)	animal/pet
un anniversaire	birthday
*le beau-père	step-father, father-in-law
le bébé	baby
le caissier	check-out operator
le camarade (de classe)	(class) mate
le chat	cat
le chauffeur	driver
le cheval (pl: chevaux)	horse
les cheveux (pl)	hair
le chien	dog
le cobaye/ cochon d'Inde	guinea-pig
le copain	friend/mate
le correspondant	pen-friend
*le demi-frère	half-brother, step-brother
*le dessinateur	designer
un employé de bureau	office worker
un enfant	child
le facteur	postman
le fils	son
le frère	brother
le garçon	boy
le grand-père	grandfather
les grands-parents (pl)	grandparents
le jumeau	twin
le lapin	rabbit
le mari	husband
le mouton	sheep
le neveu	nephew
le nom/ le nom de famille	(sur)name
un oiseau	bird
un oncle	uncle
*un ouvrier	workman
le papa	daddy
les parents (pl)	parents
le père	father
le perroquet	parrot
le poisson (rouge)	(gold) fish
le prénom	first name
le professeur	teacher
le troisième âge	old age
le vendeur	salesman
le voisin	neighbour
les yeux (pl)	eyes
une amie	friend
l'amitié	friendship
la barbe	beard
*la belle-mère	step-mother, mother-in-law
la copine	friend

la demi-sœur	half-sister, step-sister	âgé(e)	old/aged
la famille	family	aîné(e)	older
la femme	wife/woman	bon(ne)	good
la fille	daughter/girl	bouclé(e)	curly
la grand-mère	grandmother	cadet(ette)	younger
la jumelle	twin	célibataire	unmarried
les lunettes (pl)	glasses	châtain(e)	chestnut
la mère	mother	compréhensif(ive)	understanding
la naissance	birth	content(e)	happy
la nièce	niece	décédé(e)	dead
la perruche	budgerigar	*divorcé(e)	divorced
la poule	hen	familial(e)	family/ domestic
la sœur	sister	fier(ière)	proud
la souris	mouse	frisé(e)	curly
la tante	aunt	gentil(le)	nice/kind
la tortue	tortoise	marié(e)	married
		marrant(e)	amusing
s'appeler	to be called	marron	brown
bouleverser	to upset/distress	meilleur(e)	best
énerver	to get on (someone's) nerves	mignon(ne)	cute
		reconnaissant(e)	grateful
épouser	to marry	retraité(e)	retired
habiter	to live (in)	*séparé(e)	separated
se marier	to get married	sérieux(ieuse)	serious (minded)
naître	to be born		
présenter	to introduce	unique (fils unique)	only (only son)
taquiner	to tease		
travailler (comme/dans)	to work (as/in)		
vivre	to live		

1 Fill in the missing consonants in the following words.

a o _ _ _ e   d _ a _ i

b _ e _ e u   e _ i _ _

c _ e _ _ e

2 Which is the odd word out in the following lists?

a perroquet   cobaye   ouvrier   tortue   souris

b frère   naissance   fille   tante   grand-père

c agriculteur   fonctionnaire   célibataire   chauffeur   dessinatrice

d adulte   copine   sœur   poisson   ami

e anniversaire   amitié   épouser   nom   animal

3 Definitions. Who is it?

a C'est la mère de mon cousin. _____

b C'est le frère de mon père.   _____

c C'est le père de ma mère.   _____

d C'est le fils de mes parents. _____

e C'est la fille de ma sœur.   _____

4 Complete the following sentences.

a Mes _____ sont retraités.

b J'ai deux _____ mais je n'ai pas de sœurs.

c J'adore les _____; j'ai deux chiens et un chat.

d Ma mère _____ comme employée de bureau.

e Mes _____ sont divorcés.

5 Anagrams. Write out the word correctly in French. What does it mean in English?

a anipco   b spdnenrtocaro   c nérpmo   d ilmerule   e tletunse

6 Put each of these words in the correct column.

un agent de police la demi-sœur le caissier le chat le chauffeur
le cheval la nièce le demi-frère le facteur le lapin le mari
le poisson rouge l'employée de bureau la souris la tante

Animal	Travail	Famille

7 Complete the across squares with five pets, and you'll find another one down.

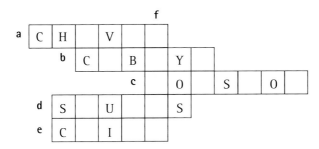

8 Fill in the blanks in this letter using the words below.

anniversaire   ans   appelle   appelle   bonjour

cheveux   frère   mignon   sœur   yeux

_____. Je m'_____ Marie. J'ai 15 _____. Mon

_____ est le 13 mai. J'ai une _____. Elle a les _____

bleus et les _____ châtain. J'ai aussi un _____. Il

s'_____ Antoine. Il est _____.

un arbre	tree	le nuage	cloud
un arrêt (d'autobus)	(bus) stop	*l'ombre	shade
*un arrondissement	district (in city)	un orage	storm
un autobus	bus	*le passage à niveau	level crossing
le bâtiment	building	*le passage clouté	pedestrian crossing
le bord de la mer	seaside		
le brouillard	fog	le paysage	scenery
le car	coach (bus)	le périphérique	ring road
*le carrefour	crossroads	le piéton	pedestrian
le centre-ville	town centre	*le port de plaisance	yacht marina
*le champ	field	le quartier	district
le château	castle/stately home	le soleil	sun
		le temps	weather
*le chemin	road/path	le touriste	tourist
le ciel	sky	le trajet	journey
*le citadin	city dweller	*le vacancier	holiday-maker
le climat	climate		
*le coucher du soleil	sunset	le vent	wind
		*le vignoble	vineyard
*un éclair	flash of lightning		
un endroit	place	*une agglomération	built-up area
*les environs	surroundings	une averse	shower
*l'espace	space	la banlieue	suburb
un habitant	inhabitant	la bibliothèque	library
l'hôtel de ville	town hall	la boutique	(small) shop
le jardin public	park	la brume	mist
le jardin zoologique	zoo	la campagne	country(side)
le jet d'eau	fountain	la cathédrale	cathedral
le lever du soleil	sunrise	*la chaleur	heat
le magasin	shop	la circulation	traffic
(le grand magasin)	(department store)	la colline	hill
		une éclaircie	sunny period
le marché	market	une église	church
le métro	underground	la ferme	farm
le musée	museum	la fontaine	fountain

la gare	(train) station	il fait du soleil	the weather is sunny
la gare routière	bus station	il gèle	it's freezing
*la grêle	hail	il neige	it's snowing
*l'herbe	grass	pleuvoir	to rain
la mairie	town hall	il pleut	it's raining
la mer	sea	Quel temps fait-il?	What's the weather like?
la météo	weather forecast		
la motocyclette	motorcycle	*se refroidir	to grow cold
la neige	snow	stationner	to park
la place	square (in town)	*tonner	to thunder
la plage	beach		
la pluie	rain	agréable	pleasant
la rivière	river	*brumeux(euse)	misty
la route	(main) road	bruyant(e)	noisy
la rue	street	couvert(e)	overcast
*la vendange	grape harvest	*doux/douce	mild
la ville	town	ennuyeux(euse)	boring
la ville jumelée	twinned town	ensoleillé(e)	sunny
*la zone piétonne	pedestrian precinct	*entouré(e) de	surrounded by
		historique	historic
		*humide	humid/damp
		industriel(le)	industrial
		*lourd(e)	heavy/sultry
avoir chaud	to be hot/warm	magnifique	magnificent
avoir froid	to be cold	mauvais(e)	bad
*briller	to shine	*orageux(euse)	stormy
*s'éclaircir	to brighten up	pauvre	poor
il fait ...	the weather is ...	pittoresque	picturesque
il fait beau	the weather is fine	riche	rich
		*sec/sèche	dry
il fait mauvais	the weather is bad	souvent	often
		tranquil(le)	quiet
il fait du brouillard	the weather is foggy	*urbain(e)	urban
		vieux/vieille	old
il fait du vent	the weather is windy		

1 Which is the odd word out in the following lists?

a   le touriste   un habitant   le bâtiment   le piéton

b   le musée   une église   l'hôtel de ville   le centre-ville

c   la route   la rue   la circulation   le soleil

d   le temps   un orage   la météo   le trajet

2 Write in the vowels to complete these words.

a   le   c _ l l _ g _   **c**   une f _ n t _ _ n _

b   la   p l _ c _   **d**   des n _ _ g _ s

3 Complete this star puzzle.

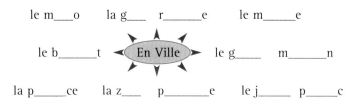

     le m___o   la g___ r_____e   le m_____e

     le b_____t ◄ En Ville ► le g____ m_____n

    la p_____ce   la z___ p_____e   le j____ p____c

4 Complete the following weather phrases by solving the anagrams.

a   Il fait du oliubrldar.   **c**   Il fait uvamisa.

b   Il ingee.   **d**   Il tupel.

5 Choose an adjective from this list to complete each blank.

vieille   vieux   bruyant   historique   industrielle

a   une _____ ville   **d**   un monument _____

b   un quartier _____   **e**   un _____ bâtiment

c   une grande ville _____

6 Sort the following words into three lists.

le train   le marché   la gare   le château   le musée   la boutique
le trajet   le jardin zoologique

Magasins	Chemin de fer	La ville

7 Fill in the blanks in this poster. Choose the words from the following list.

mer   magasins   ville   musées   boutiques   magnifique
piétonne   touristes   cathédrale

Bordeaux est une très grande _____. Dans la

zone _____ il y a beaucoup de _____

et aussi des grands _____. Pour les

_____ il y a des _____ et la

_____. Aux alentours, vous trouverez un

paysage _____. Enfin, la _____ est à

quelques kilomètres.

8 Write the names of

a trois bâtiments qui commencent par la lettre C

b cinq mots pour décrire le temps

c cinq choses qu'on trouve à la campagne.

l'allemand	German	*un internat	boarding school
l'anglais	English	le livre	(text) book
le bac(calauréat)	A-level equivalent	le lycée	(sixth form) college
le bic	biro	*le magnétophone	tape recorder
*le blanco	tippex pen	le magnétoscope	video recorder
*le brevet	GCSE (equivalent)	le moniteur	monitor
le cahier	exercise book	*le niveau	level
le cartable	satchel	un ordinateur	computer
le CES (college d'enseignement secondaire)	secondary school	le papier	paper
le collège	(secondary) school	*le principal	headteacher
		le programme	syllabus
*le concierge	caretaker	*le proviseur	headteacher
le conseiller (d'orientation)	(careers) adviser	le sac à dos	backpack
*le couloir	corridor	le stylo	pen
le cours	lesson	le surveillant	prefect, supervisor
le crayon	pencil	le tableau	board
*le débat	debate	le taille-crayon	pencil-sharpener
le dessin	art		
les devoirs (pl)	homework	le terrain de sport	sports ground
*le diplôme	diploma	le trimestre	term
le directeur	headteacher	*le vestiaire	changing room
*un effaceur	eraser pen		
un élève	pupil	la biologie	biology
un emploi du temps	timetable	la calculatrice	calculator
l'enseignement	teaching	la cantine	dining-hall
l'espagnol	Spanish	la chimie	chemistry
un examen	examination	une école (primaire)	(primary) school
*un examen blanc	mock examination	l'EMT	craft/CDT
le français	French	*l'encre	ink
le gymnase	gym(nasium)	une épreuve	test
un instituteur	(primary) teacher	l'EPS (éducation physique et sportive)	PE/games

*une excursion scolaire	school trip	apprendre	to learn
la faute	mistake	*assister à	to attend
la géographie	geography	bavarder	to chat
la gomme	rubber	dessiner	to draw
l'histoire	history	détester	to hate
l'informatique	IT	*échouer à un examen	to fail an exam
une institutrice	(primary) teacher	emprunter	to borrow
la langue	language	s'ennuyer	to get bored
la leçon	lesson	*enseigner	to teach
les mathématiques (pl) (les maths)	mathematics	étudier	to study
		*faire une expérience	to do an experiment
la matière	subject	*passer (un examen)	to take (an exam)
la monitrice	monitor		
*la pause	break	poser	to put
la physique	physics	poser (une question)	to ask (a question)
la récréation (récré)	break		
la règle	ruler	préférer	to prefer
la religion	religion	prêter	to lend
la rentrée	start of school year	*réussir à un examen	to pass an exam
la retenue	detention	*réviser	to revise
la réunion	meeting	*sécher les cours	to skive
la salle (de classe)	(class) room	*tricher	to cheat
la salle des professeurs	staff room		
les sciences naturelles (pl)	science	casse-pieds	a pain
		difficile	difficult
*la tâche	task	facile	easy
la technologie	technology	fort(e) (en)	good (at)
*la traduction	translation	intéressant(e)	interesting
*la trousse	pencil case	mixte	mixed
		préféré(e)	favourite
adorer	to adore	sévère	strict
aimer	to like	stressé(e)	stressed
		sympa	nice, friendly

1 Complete the across squares with five school subjects, and you'll find another one down.

a C'est une science.

d On étudie le passé.

b Langue parlée en France.

e On fait du sport.

c On travaille avec un ordinateur.

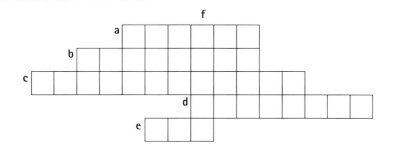

2 Which is the odd one out in the following lists?

a espagnol   allemand   anglais   dessin   français

b directeur   conseiller d'orientation   enseignement   élève   surveillant

c rentrée   faute   trimestre   cours   heure

d cantine   salle de classe   cartable   laboratoire   gymnase

e informatique   EPS   devoirs   chimie   sciences

3 Look at the illustrations and fill in the missing words.

Dans la _____ il y a un _____, une _____, une_____, une _____ et un _____.

4 Choose one of the following to complete each sentence.

| neuf heures | 15h30 | 10 minutes | une heure |

a Les cours commencent à ....

b La pause de midi dure ....

c Il y a une récré de ....

d Les cours finissent à....................

5 Identify these classroom objects and write the missing letters.

a le _ _ _ _ _ _ _ p h o n e   **b** le _ _ _ _ e a u   **c** le p _ _ _ _ r

6 Put these words into two lists, positive and negative.

retenue   difficile   nul   fort   sympa   sévère
ennuyeux   intéressant

Positif	Négatif

7 Put an appropriate verb into each sentence.

| passe | prêter | bavarder | dessine |

a J'aime _____ avec mes copines.

b L'institutrice _____ au tableau.

c Mon frère _____ son baccalauréat.

d Tu peux me _____ un stylo?

un agriculteur	farmer
un apprenti	apprentice
un apprentissage	apprenticeship
*l'autorisation	permission
l'avenir (à l'avenir)	future (in the future)
les bijoux (pl)	jewellery
le boulot	work/job (slang)
le chômage (au chômage)	unemployment (unemployed)
le chômeur	unemployed person
le client	customer
le comptable	accountant
le droit	(study of) law
un expéditeur	removal agent
*le fonctionnaire	civil servant
le gendarme	police officer
les graffitis (pl)	graffiti
*le gréviste	striker
un homme d'affaires	businessman
un ingénieur	engineer
le maçon	builder
le maquillage	make-up
le mécanicien	mechanic
le métier	job/profession
le patron	boss
le plombier	plumber
le projet	plan
le résumé	report
le salaire	salary
le stagiaire	trainee
*le syndicaliste	trade union member
le tourisme	tourism
le vandalisme	vandalism

la boucle d'oreille	earring
la candidature	application
la carrière	career
la connaissance	knowledge
*la contrôle	assessment
(école) de garçons/ de filles	boys'/girls' (school)
une école maternelle	nursery school
une équipe	team
les études (pl)	studies
l'expérience	experience
*la formation personnelle	vocational training
*la formation professionnelle	professional training
les grandes vacances	summer holidays
la licence	(university) degree
la médecine	medicine
la note	mark
*la rémunération	pay
*la sécurité	security/safety
la terminale	upper sixth
l'université	university
la violence	violence

*acquérir de l'expérience	to gain experience	expérimenté(e)	experienced
*s'adresser à	to contact	inutile	useless
*calculer	to calculate	*mixte	mixed
chercher	to look for	payé(e) (bien/mal payé(e))	paid (well/badly paid)
continuer	to continue		
écrire	to write	polyvalent(e)	versatile
embaucher	to employ/hire	privé(e)	private
encourager	to encourage	professionnel(le)	professional
envoyer	to send	public (publique)	public
faire un stage	to do a course	qualifié(e)	qualified
gagner	to earn	sans	without
mériter	to deserve	satisfaisant(e)	satisfactory
perfectionner	to improve	scientifique	scientific
poser sa canditature	to apply	sûr(e)	safe/secure
		tôt	early
protéger	to protect	utile	useful
rencontrer	to meet		
téléphoner (à)	to telephone		

à durée déterminée	fixed-term (contract)
à l'étranger	abroad
à la mode	fashionable
(assez) bien	(quite) well
avec	with
chic	smart
content(e)	pleased
démodé(e)	outdated
différent(e)	different
en plein air	in the open air
enrichissant(e)	rewarding

1 Complete this grid.

Masculin	Féminin
a	apprentie
b	mécanicienne
c	cliente
d	patronne
comptable	e

2 Find the odd one out.

a Which of these words would you not expect to find in a job advert?

cherche   téléphoner   salaire   envoyer   mal payé

b Which of these words would you not expect to find in a job application?

candidature   responsabilité   boucle d'oreille   résultats   connaissance

3 Put these words into two lists – positive or negative.

chômage   violence   bien qualifié   bien payé   sûr   démodé

Positif	Négatif

4 Fill in the missing letters to find five words related to education and training.

a une l _ _ e _ c _   **d** le t _ _ r _ _ m _

b un s _ a _ i _ i _ e   **e** mes é _ u _ e _

c la _ é _ e _ i _ e

5 Fill in the missing verbs.

| perfectionner | continuer | envoyer | gagner | rencontrer |

a Je vais _____ mes études.

b Je veux _____ le public.

c J'ai l'intention de _____ mon français.

d Je vais vous _____ une lettre.

e Vous n'allez pas _____ un gros salaire.

6 Complete these words. They are things that may not be allowed at school!

a le m _ _ _ _ _ _ _ _

b les b _ _ _ _ _

c le v _ _ _ _ _ _ _ _

7 Definitions. Who is it?

a Il construit les maisons.

b Il répare les automobiles.

c Elle dessine les maisons.

d Il n'a pas d'emploi.

e Il travaille à la ferme.

8 Find the profession by solving the anagrams.

a eginnérui   d plombtace

b molperbi   e endgamer

c çoman

un aéroglisseur	hovercraft	*le réseau	motorway
un aéroport	airport	autoroutier	network
un aller-retour	return ticket	le retard	delay
un aller simple	single	*le siège	seat
*l'atterrissage	landing	*le stationnement	parking
un avion	plane	le supplément	extra charge
les bagages (pl)	luggage	le taxi	taxi
le bateau	boat	le TGV	high-speed
*le bateau à moteur	motor boat		train
*le bateau à rames	rowing boat	les transports (pl)	public transport
le billet	ticket	en commun	
le buffet	refreshment	*les travaux	roadworks
	room	le vélo	bike
le chauffeur de taxi	taxi driver	le vélomoteur	moped
le chemin de fer	railway	*le virage	bend in road
*le coffre	car boot	le vol	flight
*le compartiment	compartment	le voyageur	passenger
*le conducteur	driver	le wagon-lit	sleeping-car
le contrôleur	ticket checker		
le départ	departure	*une aire de	picnic area
*le deux-roues	two-wheeler	pique-nique	
*l'embarquement	boarding	*une aire de repos	motorway
les feux (pl) (rouges)	traffic lights		services
*le filet	luggage rack	l'arrivée	arrival
le gazole	diesel	une auto	car
le guichet	ticket office	une autoroute	motorway
*un horaire	timetable	(la A6)	(the M6)
le métro	underground	*la bagnole	car (slang)
	train	la bicyclette	bicycle
le parking	car park	la carte	map
*le péage	toll	la ceinture de	seat-belt
le quai	platform	sécurité	
le rapide	express	la circulation	traffic
les renseignements	information	la consigne	left luggage
(pl)		(automatique)	(locker)
le RER	fast commuter	la correspondance	connection
	train service	la couchette	bed (on train)
	(Paris)	*la déviation	diversion

l'essence	petrol
la gare	train station
la gare routière	bus station
*les heures de pointe	rush hour
*la limitation de vitesse	speed limit
la moto	motorbike
la piste	runway
la place	seat
la porte	(departure) gate (at airport)
la portière	door (of car/bus/train etc)
la réservation	reservation
la route nationale	main (A) road
la salle d'attente	waiting room
la SNCF	French railways
la sortie (No6)	motorway exit (No6)
la station-service	petrol station
*la traversée	crossing
*la voie	track
la voiture	car

s'arrêter	to stop
arriver	to arrive
attendre	to wait
atterrir	to land (plane)
changer	to change
composter	to punch (ticket)
conduire	to drive
*déclarer	to declare
décoller	to take off (plane)
*dépasser	to exceed
descendre de	to get off

*doubler	to overtake
faire de l'autostop	to hitch-hike
faire le plein	to fill up (with petrol)
il faut	(you) have to
*freiner	to apply brakes
manquer	to miss
monter dans	to get on
partir	to leave
prendre	to catch
réserver	to book
*retarder	to delay
rouler (à 130km/h)	to travel (at 80 mph)
*tomber en panne	to break down
voyager	to travel

*accès interdit	no entry
à destination de	going to
*agité(e)	rough
direct(e)	direct/non-stop
direction ...	in the direction of ...
en (voiture, etc)	by (car, etc)
en provenance de	coming from
première/deuxième classe	first/second class
prochain(e)	next
sans plomb	lead free
votre attention	your attention

1 Which is the odd word out in the following lists?

a voiture   auto   taxi   carte   bagnole

b route nationale   circulation   station-service   sans plomb   aéroport

c vélo   avion   moto   vélomoteur   bicyclette

d quai   feux rouges   wagon-lit   guichet   consigne

e aéroglisseur   bateau   circulation   avion   vélo

f aller-retour   bicyclette   voie   consigne   aller simple

2 Complete the following places connected with travel.

a l' _ _ _ _ port

b la _ _ _ _ routière

c la _ _ _ _ _ _ _ -service

d une _ _ _ _ de repos

e les _ _ _ _ _ _ _ _ _ _ _ _ _ commun

3 Put these words and phrases in the appropriate columns.

composter votre billet   deuxième classe   essence   faire le plein
virage   piste   porte No8   sans plomb   couchette   vol AF218

Gare	Aéroport	Route

4 Solve the clues.

a En voiture, il faut mettre la _ _ _ _ _ _ _ _ _ _ _ _ _ _ _ _ _ _.

b Sur l' _ _ _ _ _ _ _ _ _ _ on peut rouler à 130km/h.

c On laisse les bagages à la _ _ _ _ _ _ _ _.

d Ce train est _ _ _ _ _ _. Il ne faut pas changer.

e C'est l'autoroute A10, _ _ _ _ _ _ No13.

5 Find the opposites to complete the table.

à destination de	**a**
b	arrivée
aller simple	**c**
d	descendre de
e	atterrir

6 Find a French word to fit each of the clues.

a Lots of cars, lorries etc.

b To book a seat in advance.

c Where you can sleep on a train.

d Getting off one train to catch another.

e A higher price you have to pay on some trains.

7 Solve the clues and find five kinds of transport.

a This crosses the water.

b So does this, on a cushion of air.

c This shows you how to get there.

d A convenient but expensive way to get about

e Boeing, Lockheed, Concorde.

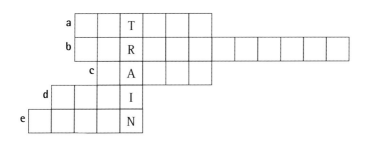

le carrefour	crossroads	à gauche	(on the) left
le cinéma	cinema	la deuxième à gauche	second left
le coin	corner	à (cent) mètres	(100) metres away
le commissariat	police station	à pied	on foot
les feux (pl) (rouges)	traffic lights	à sens unique	one way
*le fleuve	river	après	after
un hôtel	hotel	avant	before
le palais	palace	derrière	behind
*le panneau	sign	devant	in front of/ outside
le pont	bridge		
le rond-point	roundabout	en face de	opposite
		entre ... et ...	between ... and ...
la banque	bank		
la bibliothèque	library	Excusez-moi	Excuse me
la pharmacie	chemist's	jusqu'à	as far as
la rue	street	juste	just
les toilettes (pl)	toilets	(C'est) loin (?)	(Is it) far (?)
		Où se trouve ...	where is ...
aller	to go	Pardon	Excuse me
continuer	to continue	Pour aller à ...	How do I get to ...
dehors	outside	près d'ici	nearby
il y a	there is	tout droit	straight on
loin	far	tout près	nearby
prendre	to take		
proche	close	Allez ...	Go ...
tourner	to turn	Continuez ...	Carry on ...
traverser	to cross	Passez ...	Pass ...
se trouver	to be (situated)	Prenez ...	Take ...
		Tournez ...	Turn ...
à côté de	next to	Traversez ...	Cross ...
à droite	(on the) right		
la première à droite	first right		

1 In each sentence, replace the symbols with the appropriate French words or phrases.

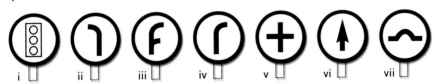

i ii iii iv v vi vii

a Aux .... tournez à ....

b Prenez la ....

c Tournez à .... au ....

d Continuez .... et traversez le ....

2 Look at this picture, then complete the sentences.

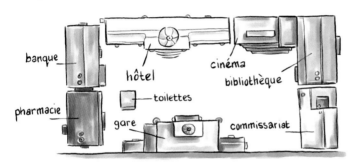

banque
hôtel
cinéma
bibliothèque
toilettes
pharmacie
gare
commissariat

a La bibliothèque est _ _ _ _ _ _ _ _ la banque.

b Le commissariat est _ _ _ _ _ _ _ la bibliothèque.

c L'hôtel est _ _ _ _ _ le cinéma et la banque.

d Il y a des toilettes _ _ _ _ _ _ la pharmacie.

3 Find the opposites to complete the table.

devant	a
b	après
près d'ici	c
à droite	d

l'accueil	reception	*le téléphérique	ski lift
*l'alpinisme	mountaineering	*le télésiège	ski lift
un appareil photo	camera	le tour (du monde)	(world) tour
l'après-midi	afternoon	*le vacancier	holiday maker
l'automne	autumn	*le voyage à forfait	package holiday
le ballon (de foot)	(foot) ball	*le voyage organisé	package holiday
*le caméscope	video-camera		
le dépliant	leaflet	une activité	activity
l'été	summer	une animatrice	play leader
le feu d'artifice	firework display	*la baignade	bathing
le groupe	group	la balle (de tennis)	(tennis) ball
l'hiver	winter	la campagne	country(side)
le lac	lake	la chaleur	heat
le matin	morning	la colonie de vacances	children's holiday camp
le moniteur	instructor	la côte	coast
un office de tourisme	tourist office	la crème (solaire)	(sun) cream
le parc	park	la distraction	entertainment
le paysage	scenery	une entrée	admission/ entrance
le pique-nique	picnic		
le printemps	spring	une excursion	excursion/trip
le sable	sand	la grotte	cave/grotto
le scooter de mer	jet-ski	les heures (pl) (d'ouverture)	(opening) times
le séjour	stay	la liste	list
le ski nautique	water-skiing	les lunettes de soleil (pl)	sunglasses
le soir	evening		
les sports (pl) (d'hiver/ nautiques)	sports (winter/ water)	*la marée basse	low tide
		*la marée haute	high tide
*le surveillant de plage	lifeguard	la montagne	mountain
		la nuit	night
le syndicat d'initiative	tourist office	la pellicule	film (for camera)

la photo(graphie)	photo(graph)	(non) accompagné(e)	(un) accompanied
la planche (à voile)	windsurfing, windsurfing-board	(pas) admis	(not) admitted
*la randonnée	walking/ rambling	compris(e)	included
		de ... à ...	from (time) to (time)
*la remontée mécanique	ski lift	du ... au ...	from (date) to (date)
la saison	season	fermé(e)	closed
*la télécabine	ski lift	gratuit(e)	free (of charge)
la tour (Eiffel)	(Eiffel) tower	guidé(e)	guided
la valise	(suit) case	moins de (10 ans)	under/ less than (10)
la visite	visit		
la vue	view	ouvert(e) (de ... à)	open (from ... to)

se baigner	to bathe/go in the water	payant(e)	to be paid for
se bronzer	to tan/go brown	toute l'année	all the year round
défaire ses valises	to unpack	toutes les demi-heures/vingt minutes	every half-hour/ twenty minutes
se détendre	to relax		
faire ses bagages	to pack		
louer	to hire		
*partir en vacances de neige	to go on a skiing holiday		
prendre un bain de soleil	to sunbathe		
se reposer	to rest		
supporter (je ne supporte pas la chaleur)	to stand (I can't stand the heat)		
visiter	to visit		
voir	to see		

1 Find the opposites and complete the table.

gratuit	a
b	fermé
matin	c
été	d

2 Put the following activities in the appropriate column.

alpinisme   vacances de neige   ski   natation   sports d'hiver
ski nautique   plongée sous-marine   excursion   planche à voile

Au bord de la mer	En montagne	Mer ou montagne

3 Which is the odd word out in the following lists?

a nuit   appareil photo   valise   lunettes de soleil   pellicule

b montagne   côte   lac   campagne   après-midi

c randonnée   pique-nique   excursion   balle   visite

d accueil   syndicat d'initiative   parc   office de tourisme
agence de voyages

e printemps   été   soir   automne   hiver

4 Fill in the missing vowels to find five things you might do on holiday.

a p _ q _ _ - n _ q _ _   **d** _ x c _ r s _ _ n

b v _ s _ t _   **e** _ l p _ n _ s m _

c b _ _ n d _ s _ l _ _ l

5 Find the French words for the following in this wordsearch.

rambling   admission   tower   to tan   scenery   coast

group   video-camera   stay   water- (le ski ....)   heat

R	A	N	D	O	N	N	E	E
C	P	A	Y	S	A	G	E	T
C	H	A	L	E	U	R	N	O
O	Z	U	I	J	T	O	T	U
T	W	U	J	O	I	U	R	R
E	S	K	D	U	Q	P	E	A
G	H	N	X	R	U	E	E	M
B	R	O	N	Z	E	R	Q	R
C	A	M	E	S	C	O	P	E

6 Look at this advert for a museum, then complete the English sentences.

MUSEE DU FROMAGE

ouverte toute l'année

entrée **65F**/10 euros
(gratuite pour les moins de 12 ans
accompagnés d'un adulte)

les chiens ne sont pas admis

visites guidées toutes les demi-heures

---

a The museum is open ....

b Children under 12 do not have to .... if they are
....

c Dogs are not ....

d There is a guided tour every ....

le balcon	balcony
le bar	bar
le bloc sanitaire	shower block
le camping	campsite
*le confort	comfort
le déjeuner	lunch
le dentifrice	toothpaste
le dîner	evening meal
un emplacement	site (on a campsite)
le gaz	gas
un gîte	holiday home
un hôtel	hotel
le (grand) lit	(double) bed
*le locataire	tenant
le luxe	luxury
*le matelas pneumatique	airbed
le mois (de juin)	month (of June)
un ouvre-boîte	can-opener
un ouvre-bouteille	bottle-opener
le passeport	passport
le petit déjeuner	breakfast
*le poêle	stove
*le porteur	porter
le réceptionniste	receptionist
le robinet	tap
le sac de couchage	sleeping bag
le savon	soap
le tarif	price-list
*le tire-bouchon	corkscrew

une alimentation	food-shop
l'animation	entertainment
une auberge de jeunesse	youth hostel
la brosse à dents	toothbrush
la caravane	caravan
la carte	card
la chambre	(bed)room
la chambre de famille	family room
la clé	key
la couverture	blanket
la demi-pension	half-board
double	double (room)
la douche	shower
l'eau (chaude/froide)	(hot/cold) water
*une écurie	stable
une étoile	star
la fiche	form
la glace	ice
la lampe (de poche)	(pocket) torch
la location	hire
la note	bill (at hotel)
la pension complète	full-board
la pièce d'identité	ID
la place	space, room
les plats cuisinés à emporter	take-away meals
la poubelle	dustbin
*la prise (de courant)	power point
la quinzaine	fortnight
la réception	reception

la réservation	reservation
*la résidence secondaire	second home
la salle de jeux	games room
la semaine	week
la serviette	towel
la tente	tent

confirmer	to confirm
descendre dans (un hôtel)	to stay in (a hotel)
dormir	to sleep
faire la cuisine	to cook
faire du camping	to go camping
fermer	to close
fonctionner	to work
garer	to park
*héberger	to accommodate
loger	to lodge
marcher	to work
répondre	to reply
rester	to stay
servir	to serve

animé(e)	lively/with entertainment
bon marché	cheap
chauffé(e)	heated
(pas) cher (chère)	(not) expensive
complet (complète)	full (up)
libre	vacant, free

ombragé(e)	shady
par écrit	in writing
par nuit	per night
par personne	per person
(non) potable	(not) drinking water
pour ... personne(s)	for ... people
*privé(e)	private
(quatre) étoiles	(four) star (restaurant/ hotel)
quinze jours	fortnight
sale	dirty
typique	typical
vers (...h)	about (... o'clock)

1 Where shall we stay? Look at the following definitions.

a Maison qu'on loue, généralement à la campagne.

b Logement pour les jeunes – pas cher!

c Terrain pour les tentes et les caravanes.

d On descend ici si on veut le confort.

2 Complete these articles you would need on a camping holiday.

a l _ m p _ d _ p _ c h _

b p _ _ l _

c m _ t _ l _ s

d _ _ v r _ - b _ _ t _

e _ _ c _ e _ _ _ c h _ g _

3 Put the following in the appropriate columns.

bloc sanitaire   chambre de famille   demi-pension   gaz
grand lit   emplacement   sac de couchage

Hôtel	Camping

4 Find five words which end in ...tion. What do they mean?

5 What is it ? Find the French word or phrase which fits each of these definitions.

a Somewhere to plug in your electrical equipment.

b Document to prove your identity – a passport or a driving licence, for example.

c Take-away meals.

d A stay at a hotel which includes all your meals.

6 Which is the odd word/phrase out in each of these lists?

a camping   gîte   passeport   auberge de jeunesse   hôtel

b emplacement   sac de couchage   gaz   bloc sanitaire   pièce d'identité

c quatre étoiles   sale   ombragé   de luxe   tout confort

d savon   serviette   poêle   brosse à dents   dentifrice

7 You receive a letter from a campsite. Some of the words are unclear. What are they?

a Notre tarif est de 10 euros par p............................ par nuit.

b La l............................ de sacs de c............................ est possible à l'accueil.

c Il y a une piscine ch............................ .

d Le camping est très a............................é.

e Veuillez c............................ votre réservation par é............................ .

8 Find the missing verb(s) in each sentence.

a Ma mère veut d.................... dans un hôtel, car elle n'aime pas ....
la cuisine.

b Où est-ce que je peux g.................... ma voiture ?

c Je veux r.................... une semaine.

d L'eau chaude ne m.................... pas.

le Canada	Canada	l'Afrique	Africa
le Danemark	Denmark	l'Allemagne	Germany
les Etats-Unis (pl)	United States	les Alpes (pl)	Alps
le Japon	Japan	l'Amérique	America
*le Maroc	Morocco	l'Angleterre	England
le Massif Central	Central mountain range in France	l'Autriche	Austria
		la Belgique	Belgium
		la Bretagne	Brittany (region)
le Midi	South of France		
les Pays-Bas (pl)	Netherlands	la Corse	Corsica
le pays de Galles	Wales	l'Ecosse	Scotland
le Portugal	Portugal	l'Espagne	Spain
le Québec	Quebec (French -speaking area of Canada)	l'Europe	Europe
		la France	France
		la Grande-Bretagne	Great Britain
le Rhin	(river) Rhine	la Grèce	Greece
le Rhône	(river) Rhône	la Hollande	Holland
le Royaume-Uni	United Kingdom	l'Irlande (du Nord)	(Northern) Ireland
le continent	continent	l'Italie	Italy
le département	French equivalent of English county	la Manche	(English) Channel
		la Méditerranée	Mediterranean
le douanier	customs officer	la Normandie	Normandy (region)
un étranger	foreigner		
le gouvernement	government	les Pyrénées (pl)	Pyrenees
un habitant	inhabitant	la Russie	Russia
le monde	world	la Suède	Sweden
un océan	ocean	la Suisse	Switzerland
le pays	country	l'UE	European Union
le président	president	la communauté	community
le roi	king	la commune	district/village

la douane	customs	italien(ne)[1]	Italian
la frontière	frontier	japonais(e)[1]	Japanese
la langue	language	portugais(e)[1]	Portuguese
la nationalité	nationality	russe[1]	Russian
la population	population	suédois(e)[1]	Swedish
la région	region	suisse	Swiss
la reine	queen		

		à l'étranger	abroad
africain(e)	African	au	in (+ masculine country)
allemand(e)[1]	German		
américain(e)	American	aux	in (+ plural countries)
anglais(e)[1]	English		
autrichien(ne)	Austrian	en	in (+ feminine country)
belge	Belgian	*bilingue	bilingual
britannique	British	international(e)	international
canadien(ne)	Canadian	national(e)	national
corse	Corsican	régional(e)	regional
danois(e)[1]	Danish		
écossais(e)	Scottish	Bruxelles	Brussels
espagnol(e)[1]	Spanish	Douvres	Dover
européen(ne)	European	Edimbourg	Edinburgh
flamand(e)[1]	Flemish (language spoken in Belgium)	Londres	London
		Marseille	Marseilles
français(e)[1]	French		
francophone	French-speaking		

[1 The masculine form of these adjectives is also used for the language]

gallois(e)[1]	Welsh
grec(que)[1]	Greek
hollandais(e)[1]	Dutch
indien(ne)	Indian
irlandais(e)[1]	Irish

1 Match the language with the country.

a hollandais   b gallois   c allemand   d anglais   e français

Autriche   Etats-Unis   Pays-Bas   Suisse   pays de Galles

2 Which is the odd one out in the following lists?

a l'Allemagne   la Suède   le Danemark   les Etats-Unis   la Grèce

b Londres   Douvres   Marseille   Manche   Calais

c le Midi   la Bretagne   la Normandie   l'Afrique   le Massif Central

d Bretagne   Suisse   Pyrénées   Normandie   Midi

e le Maroc   le Canada   la Suisse   l'Angleterre   la Belgique

3 Complete the following grid.

autrichien	autrichienne
écossais	a
b	américaine
grec	c
d	belge

4 Match the flag with the country.

 a
 b
 c

 d
 e
 f

Italie   Etats-Unis   Suède   Grande-Bretagne   Allemagne   France

5 Find the missing word in each of the following sentences.

nationalité Edimbourg francophone bilingue président Ecosse population

a La .... de l'Union Européenne est de 250 million d'habitants.

b En Angleterre, il y a une reine; en France, il y a un ....

c Le Maroc est un pays ....

d Thierry Henri est de .... française.

e .... est la capitale de l'.................... .

f Une personne qui parle italien et grec est ....

6 Put the following words in the correct column in the grid.

Irlande du Nord Normandie Espagne Marseille Londres Afrique
Bretagne Pyrénées Portugal Italie Ecosse Autriche Midi Bruxelles

Le Royaume-Uni	La France	L'Union Européenne	Le Monde

7 Find the missing words in each of the following sentences.

a Il est né au Danemark; il est ....

b Elle est née en Italie; elle est ....

c Il est né à Edimbourg; il est ....

d Elle est née à Douvres; elle est ....

e Il est né à Madrid; il est ....

l'argent	money	le poste (de police)	(police) station
le billet (de ... euros)	(... euros) note	le radiateur	radiator
		le sac (à main)	(hand) bag
le bureau de change	exchange bureau	le timbre (poste)	(postage) stamp
le bureau des objets trouvés	lost property office	un timbre à ... euros	a ... euro stamp
le chèque (de voyage)	(traveller's) cheque	le volant	steering wheel
*le chéquier	cheque book	la bague	ring
le code postal	postcode	la banque	bank
*le colis	parcel	la batterie	battery (in car)
l'euro	euro (currency)	BNP (Bank Nationale de Paris)	famous French bank
le formulaire	form	la boîte aux lettres	letter box
le franc	franc	la caisse	cash desk
GDF (Gaz de France)	gas company	la carte de crédit	credit card
le garage	garage	la carte (postale)	(post) card
le guichet	window (e.g. in bank)	la crevaison	puncture
l'indicatif	dialling code	EDF (Electricité de France)	electricity company
le moteur	engine	l'huile	oil
le numéro (d'immatriculation)	number (registration)	la lettre	letter
le paquet	parcel	*la levée	collection (from letter box)
le parapluie	umbrella	la livre (sterling)	pound (sterling)
le pare-brise	windscreen	la marque	make/brand
le permis de conduire	driving licence	la montre	watch
le phare	headlamp	la pièce (de ... euros)	(... euro) coin
le pneu	tyre	la poste	post office
le portable	mobile phone	PTT (Postes, Télécommunications et Télédiffusion)	French postal services
le portefeuille	wallet		
le porte-monnaie	purse	la roue	wheel

la signature	signature	Allô	Hello (on telephone)
*la télécarte	phone card		
la valeur	value	C'est le garage X?	Is that X garage?
		crevé(e)	punctured
aider	to help	dedans	inside
attendre	to wait (for)	dessus	on (it)
changer	to change	en argent	(made of) silver
composer	to dial	en cuir	(made of) leather
compter	to reckon		
contenir	to contain	en espèces	in cash
couper	to cut	en or	(made of) gold
décrire	to describe	en panne	out of order
décrocher	to lift the receiver	fermé(e) à clef	locked
dépanner	to fix/repair	Il/Elle est de quelle couleur/ marque?	What colour/ make is it?
envoyer	to send		
laisser	to leave (behind)	le/la/l'/les	it/them
		merci	thank you
oublier	to forget	Où/Quand l'avez vous perdu(e)?	Where/When did you lose it?
perdre	to lose		
remplir	to fill in/ complete	Pouvez-vous le/la/les décrire?	Can you describe it/ them?
réparer	to repair		
faire réparer	to have repaired	Pouvez-vous m'aider?	Can you help me?
retirer	to take out/ withdraw	s'il vous plaît	please
signer	to sign	valable	valid
téléphoner	to telephone		
tomber en panne	to break down		
*toucher	to cash (a cheque)		
voler	to steal		

1 Match up the halves of these sentences.

a Ma voiture est ...

b J'ai perdu une ...

c Vous devez composer ...

d Je voudrais envoyer ...

e Je voudrais changer ...

i ... le numéro.

ii ... un colis en Angleterre.

iii ... tombée en panne.

iv ... dix livres sterling.

v ... bague en or.

2 Find the French word or phrase to solve these clues.

a This document authorises you to drive.

b You carry change in it.

c The car lights won't work without it.

d You have to fill this in at the lost property office.

e You can make a phone call from anywhere with this.

3 Put these words into the correct column.

timbre   chèque   télécarte   code postal   indicatif   billet de 100 euros
livre sterling   paquet   portable   lettre

La Banque	La Poste	France Télécom

4 Find the odd word out in each of the following lists.

a euro   billet   timbre   pièce   franc

b pneu   phare   télécarte   pare-brise   roue

c billet   chèque de voyage   volant   carte de crédit   pièce

d portable   portefeuille   porte-monnaie   billet   argent

5 Complete the crossword with five items of lost property, and you will find a sixth item.

a It's exciting to receive one of these through the post.

b It stops you getting wet.

c It tells the time.

d You have to go to the Post Office to send this.

e You need it to write a cheque.

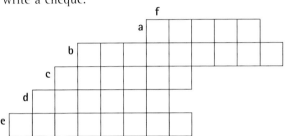

6 Fill in the missing words in these sentences.

portefeuille   signer   numéro   espèces   crevé

a Je vais payer en ....

b J'ai un pneu ....

c Voulez-vous .... ici?

d Quel est votre .... de téléphone?.

e J'ai perdu mon ....

7 Solve these anagrams. They are all words you might need when filling in a lost property form.

a isslaer   **d** criedér

b grenat   **e** drupe

c ricu

un accident (de la route)	(road) accident	*le plâtre	plaster (of Paris)
le bras	arm	*le plombage	filling
*le cabinet	doctor's surgery	*le poignet	wrist
		*le poumon	lung
*le centre hospitalier	(general) hospital	*les premiers soins	first aid
		les reins	kidneys
le cœur	heart	le rendez-vous	appointment
le comprimé	tablet	le rhume	cold
*le contrôle	check-up	*le rhume des foins	hayfever
le corps	body	*le sang	blood
le cou	neck	le sirop	(liquid) medicine
le coude	elbow		
le dentiste	dentist	le sparadrap	(sticking) plaster
le docteur	doctor		
le doigt	finger	le ventre	stomach
le dos	back	les yeux (pl)	eyes
l'estomac	stomach		
*le foie	liver	*une aspirine	aspirin
*le front	forehead	une ambulance	ambulance
le genou	knee	la bouche	mouth
un hôpital	hospital	la cheville	ankle
le mal (mal de tête) (mal aux dents)	pain (headache) (toothache)	la dent	tooth
		*la diarrhée	diarrhoea
		*la douleur	pain
le malade	patient	une épaule	shoulder
le médicament	medicine	la fièvre	temperature/ fever
le médecin	doctor		
le moustique	mosquito	la gorge	throat
le nez	nose	la grippe	flu
l'œil	eye	*une insolation	sunstroke
*le pansement	dressing	la jambe	leg
*le pharmacien	chemist	la main	hand
le pied	foot	la maladie	illness

la mort	death	garder le lit	to stay in bed
une ordonnance	prescription	*se mettre au régime	to go on a diet
une oreille	ear		
*la pilule	pill	piquer	to sting, bite
la piqûre	sting/bite	prendre	to take
la piqûre	injection	*renverser	to overturn/ upset
la police	police		
*la radio	X-ray	*respirer	to breathe
la santé	health	se reposer	to rest
la tête	head	*soigner	to care for
*la toux	cough	souffrir	to suffer
la voix	voice	tomber malade	to fall ill
		tousser	to cough
		vomir	to be sick

allumer	to light		
aller mieux	to get/feel better	Au secours!	Help!
appeler	to call	avant/après les repas	before/after meals
avoir mal à (l'oreille)	to have a pain in (the ear) (= earache)	blessé(e)	wounded/ injured
		cassé(e)	broken
avoir mal au cœur	to feel sick	(deux/trois) fois par jour	(two/three) times a day
(se) blesser	to injure (oneself)	enrhumé(e)	suffering from a cold
*se brûler la main	to burn one's hand		
*se casser (le bras)	to break (one's arm)	*faible	weak
		grave	serious
*se couper (le doigt)	to cut (one's finger)	*grièvement	seriously
		handicapé(e)	disabled
dormir	to sleep	malade	ill
se faire mal à (la jambe)	to hurt one's (leg)	mort(e)	dead
		sain(e)	healthy
*se fouler la cheville	to sprain one's ankle		

1 Find the French for these parts of the body in the wordsearch.

ankle
wrist
body
arm
eye
heart
mouth
neck
nose
stomach

G	S	C	O	U	V	R	W
F	O	E	I	L	H	D	L
C	H	E	V	I	L	L	E
R	C	O	E	U	R	N	B
B	O	U	C	H	E	E	C
B	R	A	S	Y	Q	Z	E
M	P	O	I	G	N	E	T
E	S	T	O	M	A	C	A

2 Complete these sentences with the appropriate word from this list.

ordonnance   pieds   hôpital   tête   comprimé

a Mes chaussures sont trop petites. J'ai mal aux ....

b Je vais prendre de l'aspirine. J'ai mal à la ....

c Le médecin m'a donné une ....

d Je dois prendre un .... trois fois par jour.

e Je vais à l'................... en ambulance.

3 Which of the following might be involved in a car accident?

pharmacien   toux   sang   dentiste   pansement

radio   police   douleur   rhume des foins

4 Solve the anagrams to find five things you would get from the chemist's.

  a dapspraar   **b** émicdatenm   **c** omimrpcé   **d** poirs   **e** luplie

5 Where would you go for help with the following?

rhume   jambe cassée   mal de mer   fièvre   diarrhée   grippe

Médecin	Hôpital

6 Find the French word for these definitions.

a It's usually worse when there's pollen about.

b The doctor – or a wasp – might give you this!

c Most people have ten of these.

d If this comes out, see your dentist.

e You go to the dentist with this problem, too.

7 Which is the odd word out in these lists?

a pompier   pharmacien   médecin   front   dentiste

b toux   fièvre   contrôle   rhume   mal à la gorge

c doigt   bras   main   poignet   cheville

d malade   enrhumé   blessé   faible   mort

un appartement	flat	le jardinage	gardening
un arbre	tree	le lavabo	washbasin
*le bac à linge	sink (for washing)	le lave-vaisselle	dishwasher
		le lit	bed
*le bac à vaisselle	sink (for washing-up)	le meuble	furniture
		*le miroir	mirror
le buffet	sideboard	le mur	wall
le bureau	desk	un oreiller	pillow
*le câble à péage	cable television	un ordinateur	computer
le canapé	settee	un ouvre-boîte	tin opener
*le cendrier	ashtray	un ouvre-bouteille	bottle opener
le chauffage central	central heating	*le palier	landing
le clou	nail	*le pavillon	detached house
le congélateur	freezer	le placard	cupboard
un escalier	stairs	le plafond	ceiling
l'étage	floor/storey	le plancher	floor
le premier étage	first floor	le poster	poster
le deuxième étage	second floor	le premier étage	first floor
*un évier	sink	le quartier	district
le fauteuil	armchair	le réveil	alarm clock
*le four	oven	le rez-de-chaussée	ground floor
le four à micro-ondes	microwave oven	le rideau	curtain
*le foyer	home	le robinet	tap
le frigo	fridge	le salon	living-room
le garage	garage	*le sous-sol	basement
le gaz	gas	le tapis	carpet
*le gazon	lawn	le toit	roof
*le grenier	loft	*le verger	orchard
*un immeuble	block of flats	le vestibule	hall
le jardin (potager)	(vegetable) garden	*le volet	shutter
		les WC (pl)	toilet

une adresse	address	la plante	plant
une allumette	match	la porte	door
*une antenne parabolique	satellite dish	(la porte d'entrée)	(front door)
une armoire	wardrobe	la recette	recipe
*la baignoire	bath	la route	(main) road
la cave	cellar	la salle à manger	dining-room
la chaîne stéréo/ hi-fi	stereo	la salle de bains	bathroom
la chaise	chair	la salle de séjour	sitting-room
la chambre	bedroom	*la serrure	lock
*la cheminée	chimney/ fire-place	la table	table
		*la télévision câblée	cable television
la clé	key	la terrasse	terrace/patio
*la couette	duvet	les toilettes (pl)	toilets
la cuisine	kitchen		
la cuisinière (à gaz/électrique)	cooker (gas/electric)	déménager	to move (house)
la douche	shower	donner sur	to look out onto
*une échelle	ladder	habiter	to live (in)
une entrée	entrance	partager	to share
la fenêtre	window	prêter	to lend
la fleur	flower		
*une HLM	council house/ flat	confortable	comfortable
la lampe	lamp	*de luxe	luxurious
la machine à laver	washing machine	grand(e)	big
		*jumelé(e)	semi-detached
la maison	house	*meublé(e)	furnished
la marmite	cooking pot	moderne	modern
la moquette	fitted carpet	petit(e)	small
la nappe	tablecloth	*pittoresque	picturesque
la pelouse	lawn	vieux (vieille)	old
la pièce	room		

1 Complete the labels for this house.

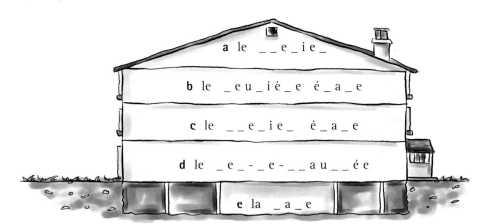

a le _ _ e _ i e _

b le _ e u _ i è _ e é _ a _ e

c le _ _ e _ i e _   é _ a _ e

d le _ e _ - _ e - _ _ a u _ _ é e

e la _ a _ e

2 Which is the odd word out in the following lists?

a mur   toit   plancher   plafond   rideau

b maison   échelle   appartement   HLM   immeuble

c moderne   petit   confortable   terrasse   vieux

d moquette   pelouse   jardin   arbre   fleur

e chambre   cuisine   salle à manger   fenêtre   salon

3 Put the following in the right rooms.

four   fauteuil   canapé   lave-vaisselle   marmite   baignoire
cuisinière   douche   congélateur   lavabo

Cuisine	Salle de bains	Salon

4 Find the French words to fit these definitions.

a You keep the car there.

b It's for washing clothes.

c You use it to get to the first floor.

d You sit round it to keep warm.

e It should wake you up in the morning.

5 Fill in the missing vowels to find five things you might find in a house.

a t _ p _ s

b _ _ v r _ - b _ _ t _

c m _ r _ _ r

d v _ s t _ b _ l _

e t _ _ l _ t t _ s

6 Complete these sentences with the missing verb.

habite	prête	donne	déménage	partage

a Sandrine, ...-moi ta clé.

b Je .... ma chambre avec mon frère.

c Elle .... dans une nouvelle maison.

d J' .... une maison en pierre.

e Ma chambre .... sur un grand jardin.

7 Solve these clues.

a On y trouve des plantes et des arbres.

b Il en faut une pour avoir la télévision par satellite.

c On y fait la vaisselle (si on n'a pas de lave-vaisselle!)

d Il en faut une pour ouvrir la porte.

l'argent de poche	pocket money	demander	to ask
un aspirateur	vacuum cleaner	(à quelqu'un)	(someone)
le déjeuner	lunch	(de faire quelque	(to do
le dîner	evening meal/	chose)	something)
	dinner	se déshabiller	to get
*le fer à repasser	iron		undressed
*le goûter	tea (snack)	devoir	to have to
le jardinage	gardening	donner	to give
*le mélo	soap (on TV)	emprunter	to borrow
le ménage	housework	entendre	to hear
*le nettoyage	clearing	*essuyer (la	to dry (the
le rasoir	razor	vaisselle)	dishes)
le repas (du soir)	(evening) meal	faire	to do
le repassage	ironing	(faire du bricolage)	(to do odd
le souper	supper		jobs)
		(faire la cuisine)	(to do the
la brosse	brush		cooking)
les courses (pl)	shopping	(faire les courses)	(to do the
la cuisine	the cooking		shopping)
la lessive	washing	(faire le repassage)	(to do the
la poubelle	dustbin		ironing)
la vaisselle	washing-up	(faire les devoirs)	(to do
			homework)
aider (quelqu'un)	to help	(faire du baby-	(to baby-sit)
	(someone)	sitting)	
aller au lit	to go to bed	(faire du jardinage)	(to do some
se brosser	to brush		gardening)
(les dents)	(one's teeth)	(faire la vaisselle)	(to do the
(les cheveux)	(one's hair)		washing-up)
se coucher	to go to bed	faire	to make
*débarrasser la table	to clear the	(faire le lit)	(to make the
	table		bed)
		il (me) faut	(I) have to
		gagner	to earn
		frapper	to knock
		s'habiller	to get dressed
		laver (la voiture)	to wash (the
			car)

se laver	to have a wash	en désordre	in a mess
se lever	to get up	en semaine	on a weekday
mettre la table	to set the table	le dimanche	on Sundays
nettoyer	to clean	le samedi	on Saturdays
passer l'aspirateur	to vacuum	ménager(ère)	household
prendre	to have	normalement	normally
(une douche)	(a shower)	partout	everywhere
(un bain)	(a bath)	quelquefois	sometimes
prendre (le petit	to have	rarement	rarely
déjeuner, etc)	(breakfast, etc)	souvent	often
préparer	to prepare	tard	late
quitter (la maison)	to leave (home)	toujours	always
ranger	to tidy/put away	tous les	every
se raser	to have a shave	(jours)	(day)
recevoir	to receive/to get	(matins)	(morning)
réveiller (quelqu'un)	to wake (someone) up	(soirs)	(evening)
se réveiller	to wake up	(week-ends)	(weekend)
sortir (la poubelle)	to take out (the dustbin)		
tenir	to hold		
*tondre (le gazon)	to mow (the lawn)		

à ... heures	at ... o'clock
à ... heures (dix)	at (ten) past...
à ... heures moins (vingt)	at (twenty) to ...
après	after
avant	before
de temps en temps	from time to time
d'habitude	usually

1 Put these everyday activities in order.

a   se coucher   se lever   se réveiller   se laver   se déshabiller

b   débarrasser la table   dîner   faire la vaisselle   mettre la table
   faire la cuisine

2 Find the French for five activities you do outside the house.

3 How often do you help at home? Fill in the missing letters.

a   s _ _ v _ _ t   d   q _ _ l q _ _ _ o i _

b   d _ t _ _ p s   e _   _ e m _ _   e   t _ _ s   l _ s   j _ _ _ s

c   t _ _ j _ _ r _

4 Find the odd word/phrase out in the following lists.

a   se laver   se réveiller   se brosser les dents   se peigner   se raser

b   rasoir   aspirateur   goûter   poubelle   fer à repasser

c   courses   repassage   vaisselle   ménage   argent de poche

d   jardinage   dîner   petit déjeuner   déjeuner   goûter

5 Fill in the blanks with the appropriate verb.

demande	me lève	range	prépare	reçois

a   En semaine je .... à 7h30, mais le week-end je fais la grasse matinée.

b   Le samedi, je .... le petit déjeuner pour ma mère.

c   Quelquefois ma mère me .... de faire les courses.

d   Si je fais la vaisselle, je .... de l'argent de poche.

e   Je .... ma chambre tous les week-ends.

6 Your mum wants help in the house. What does she tell you to do?

Fill in the missing words.

a Sors la ....!

b Débarrasse la ....!

c Fais la ....!

d Fais ton ....!

e Tonds le ....!

7 Replace the pictures in these sentences with the appropriate French word(s).

a Je passe

c Je fais

e Je fais

b Je me

d Je prends

l'anniversaire (de mariage)	birthday (wedding anniversary)	la carte (de Noël)	(Christmas) card
		la cérémonie	ceremony
le cadeau	present/gift	la chanson	song
le champagne	champagne	la coutume	custom
le chant de Noël	Christmas carol	une église	church
*le défilé	procession	une épouse	wife
un époux	husband	la fête	(saint's) name day
le feu d'artifice	firework display	la fête	festival/ celebration/ party
le fiancé	fiancé		
le gâteau (d'anniversaire)	(birthday) cake	la fête des Mères	Mother's Day
l'hymne national	national anthem	la fête du village	village fête
le jour de l'an	New Year's Day	la fête nationale	French national day (Bastille Day)
le jour de fête	holiday		
le jour de Noël	Christmas Day		
le jour de congé	day off	*la fête foraine	funfair
le jour férié	public (bank) holiday	les fiançailles	engagement (party)
le maire	mayor	*la galette des rois	Twelfth Night cake
le mariage	marriage	la mairie	town hall
*le marié	bridegroom	*la mariée	bride
un œuf	an egg	la Marseillaise	French national anthem
le père Noël	Father Christmas		
le quatorze juillet	14th July	la messe (de minuit)	(midnight) mass
le réveillon	Christmas Eve/ New Year's Eve meal	les noces (d'argent)	wedding (silver wedding anniversary)
le sapin de Noël	Christmas tree		
une alliance	wedding ring	la Saint-Nicolas	Saint Nicholas' day
la boum	party	la Saint-Sylvestre	New Year's Eve
la bûche de Noël	Yule log		

la Saint-Valentin	Saint Valentine's Day
la salle des fêtes	village hall
la surprise-partie	party
les vacances (pl) (de Pâques, etc)	(Easter etc) holidays

célébrer	to celebrate
chanter	to sing
décorer	to decorate
donner	to give
envoyer	to send
faire la bise (à)	to kiss
faire la fête	to have a party/ to have fun
*faire un paquet-cadeau	to gift-wrap
féliciter	to congratulate
fêter	to celebrate
se fiancer	to get engaged
se marier (avec)	to get married (to)
offrir	to offer
ouvrir	to open
pardonner	to forgive
recevoir	to receive
remercier	to thank
répondre	to reply
souhaiter	to wish

Bonne année!	Happy New Year!
Bon anniversaire!	Happy Birthday!
Bon appétit!	Enjoy your meal!
Bonne fête!	Happy name-day!
Bonne journée!	Have a nice day!
Bonne soirée!	Have a nice evening!
Bon voyage!	Have a good journey!
Félicitations!	Congratulations!
Joyeux Noël!	Merry Christmas
Meilleurs vœux!	Best Wishes!
Santé!	Cheers!
(à) Noël	(at) Christmas
(à) Pâques	(at) Easter
(à) la Pentecôte	(at) Whitsun

agréable	pleasant
autour de (la table)	round (the table)
beaucoup (de)	many/a lot (of)
civil(e)	civil (i.e. non-religious)
depuis (... ans)	for (... years)
(en) chocolat	(made of) chocolate
heureux (euse)	happy
marié(e)	married
religieux (euse)	religious

1 Put the appropriate festival with these dates.

   a le 14 février   **b** le 14 juillet   **c** le 25 décembre   **d** le 31 décembre

2 Which celebration do you associate these words with?

   a carte   cadeaux   boum   gâteau   âge

   b sapin   chant   messe de minuit   Père Noël   bûche

3 What do you say to someone...

   a on January 1st?

   b when they are about to start a meal?

   c when it's their birthday?

   d when they tell you they're engaged?

   e when they're off on holiday?

   f on Christmas day?

4 Fill in the missing words in these sentences.

> en chocolat   jour de congé   feu d'artifice   carte   cadeaux

   a Le jour de Noël est un .... pour la plupart de gens.

   b Le Père Noël apporte des .... pour les enfants.

   c Le 14 juillet, il y a un grand ....

   d A Pâques, on donne des œufs ....

   e A la Saint-Valentin, je donne un cadeau et une .... à ma petite amie.

5 Find the French words to fit these definitions.

   a Eaten on the 6th January.

   b This comes after 25 years of marriage.

   c What you say when you drink to someone's health.

d You send your mum a card on this day.

e It is decorated with lights and baubles.

6 Fill in the crossword, and find another word.

a French people must go here to get married.

b What you sing.

c The female half of the happy couple.

d What you say to congratulate someone.

e The other half of the couple.

f Eaten at birthday parties.

g A religious ceremony is held here.

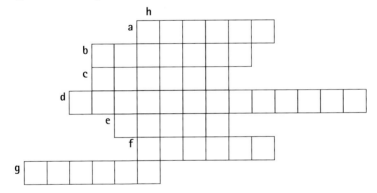

7 Fill in the missing verbs in these sentences.

| envoie | fête | ouvrir | fait la bise | recevoir |

a Demain, je .... mes 18 ans.

b J'espère que je vais .... beaucoup de cadeaux.

c J'................ des cartes à toutes mes amies.

d J'adore .... les cadeaux le jour de Noël.

e Quand on rencontre des amis, on leur ....

un abricot	apricot	le pain	bread
l'agneau	lamb	(grillé)	(toasted)
un ananas	pineapple	le pamplemousse	grapefruit
le beurre	butter	le pâté	pâté
le biscuit	biscuit	les petits pois (pl)	peas
le bœuf	beef	le poireau	leek
le bonbon	sweet	le poisson	fish
le cassis	blackcurrant	le poivre	pepper
le champignon	mushroom	le poivron (rouge)	(red) pepper
le chocolat (chaud)	(hot) chocolate	le porc	pork
le chou	cabbage	le pot	pot/jar
le chou de Bruxelles	Brussels sprouts	le potage	soup
le chou-fleur	cauliflower	le poulet	chicken
le citron	lemon	le produit	product
le concombre	cucumber	le raisin	grapes
le croissant	croissant	le riz	rice
les épinards (pl)	spinach	le rôti (de bœuf)	roast (beef)
*le foie gras	duck liver terrine	le saucisson	(salami-type) sausage
les fruits (pl)	fruit	le sel	salt
le gâteau	cake	le steak	steak
le gras	fat	le sucre	sugar
les haricots verts (pl)	green beans	le thon	tuna
		le veau	veal
le jambon	ham	le vinaigre	vinegar
le jus	sauce/gravy	le yaourt	yoghurt
le lait	milk		
le légume	vegetable	la baguette	French loaf
le miel	honey	la banane	banana
un œuf	egg	la boîte	can/tin
un oignon	onion	la carotte	carrot
		les céréales (pl)	cereal

la cerise	cherry	la saucisse	sausage
les chips (pl)	crisps	la soupe	soup
la confiture	jam	la tartine	slice of bread
la côtelette	chop	la tomate	tomato
la dinde	turkey	la viande	meat
l'eau (minérale)	(mineral) water		
la farine	flour	aimer	to like
la fraise	strawberry	ajouter	to add
la framboise	raspberry	avoir faim	to be hungry
les frites (pl)	chips	avoir soif	to be thirsty
*la gaufre	waffle	boire	to drink
la glace	ice-cream	détester	to hate
l'huile	oil	*éplucher	to peel
la laitue	lettuce	être	to be
la limonade	lemonade	manger	to eat
la moutarde	mustard	verser	to pour
la noix	walnut		
la nourriture	food	*allergique (à)	allergic (to)
une omelette	omelette	dégoûtant(e)	disgusting
une orange	orange	délicieux(euse)	delicious
les pâtes (pl)	pasta	laitier(ière)	dairy
la pâtisserie	pastry/cake	piquant(e)	spicy
la pêche	peach	salé(e)	salted/savoury
la poêle	frying pan	végétarien(ne)	vegetarian
la poire	pear		
la pomme	apple		
la pomme de terre	potato		
la purée	purée/mash		
la salade (verte)	(green) salad		
la sardine	sardine		
la sauce	sauce		

1 Put these items of food in the appropriate column.

poulet   fraise   pomme de terre   poire   agneau   bœuf   petits pois

citron   épinards   saucisson   pamplemousse   chou-fleur

Fruit	Légume	Viande

2 Find the odd word out in each of these lists:

a huile   moutarde   limonade   vinaigre   poivre

b lait   croissant   pain   beurre   baguette

c laitue   haricots verts   petits pois   chou   agneau

d viande   chocolat   riz   pommes de terre   pain

3 List these ingredients in the correct column.

œufs   poivre   sucre   cerises   oignon   champignon

pommes de terre   sel   farine   confiture

Potage	Gâteau

4 **Complete these excuses for not eating what you are offered.**

a Non merci, je n'ai pas ....

b Non merci, je suis ....

c Non merci, je n'............. pas les épinards.

d Non merci, je suis .... au poisson.

5 **Which of these items would a really strict vegetarian or a vegan not eat or drink?**

un œuf   le thon   la gaufre   les céréales   le lait   le yaourt

6 **Match the halves.**

a nourr...   i ...isson

b sauc...   ii ...boise

c côte...   iii ...ignon

d champ...   iv ...lette

e fram...   v ...iture

7 **Find six things to eat in this wordsearch.**

T	S	K	B	R	V	L	D	X
P	O	I	S	S	O	N	R	E
Q	R	M	P	D	Z	J	O	P
S	L	P	A	I	N	U	E	U
N	D	Y	R	T	R	F	U	A
B	H	U	I	L	E	N	F	C
O	I	G	N	O	N	S	S	E

l'ail	garlic
un apéritif	aperitif (drink)
le bifteck	steak
le bol	bowl
le café (-crème)	(white) coffee
le canard	duck
le casse-croûte	snack
le cidre	cider
le coca (cola)	coca-cola
le couteau	knife
le couvert	place setting
le crabe	crab
le croque-monsieur	ham & cheese toasted sandwich
le croque-madame	with fried egg on top
le dessert	dessert/pudding
un escargot	snail
le fast-food	fast food (restaurant)
le fromage	cheese
le fruit	fruit
les fruits de mer (pl)	seafood
le garçon (de café)	waiter
un hamburger	hamburger
un hors-d'œuvre	starter
le jus (de fruit)	(fruit) juice
le melon	melon
le légume	vegetable

le menu (à ... euros)	(... euro) menu
à prix fixe	fixed price
le menu enfant	children's menu
un orangina	orange drink (brand name)
le parfum	flavour
le plat	dish (food)
le plat cuisiné	take-away dish
le plat du jour	today's special
le plat principal	main course
le pourboire	tip
le restaurant	restaurant
le sandwich	sandwich
le saumon	salmon
le service	service
le steak-frites	steak and chips
le thé (au lait)	tea (with milk)
le verre	glass
le vin	wine

l'addition	bill
une assiette	plate
une assiette de crudités	assorted raw vegetables
la bière	beer
la boisson	drink
la bouteille	bottle
la cafetière	coffee pot
la carafe	jug/carafe

la carte	menu	prendre	to have (food/drink)
la cerise	cherry	servir	to serve
la charcuterie	cooked meats	se servir de	to use
la chope	mug		
la côte de porc	pork chop	à la carte	choice from menu
la crème	cream	... à la fraise (etc)	strawberry ...
la crêpe	pancake	à point	medium rare
la crêperie	pancake restaurant	bien cuit(e)	well done
la crevette	prawn	chinois(e)	Chinese
les crudités	assorted raw vegetables	(non) compris(e)	(not) included
la cuiller	spoon	garni(e)	including vegetables
une douzaine de	a dozen	inclus	included
la fourchette	fork	*libre service	self-service
la glace	ice-cream	(tarte) maison	home-made (tart)
la grillade	grilled meat	(yaourt) nature	natural/plain (yoghurt)
les huîtres (pl)	oysters	parfait	perfect
les moules (pl)	mussels	pour commencer	to start with
la pizza	pizza	propre	clean
*la soucoupe	saucer	saignant(e)	rare
la spécialité	speciality	sale	dirty
la tarte (aux pommes)	(apple) tart		
la tasse	cup	Mademoiselle!	Miss! (to waitress)
la terrasse	terrace	Monsieur!	(to call waiter)
la truite	trout	Qu'est-ce que c'est le/la ...?	What is ...?
la vanille	vanilla	C'est quoi le/la ...?	What is ...?
commander	to order		
commencer	to start/begin		
mélanger	to mix		

1 Which is the odd word out in the following lists?

a thé au lait   restaurant   café-crème   jus de pomme   bière

b truite   fruits de mer   moules   canard   saumon

c cuiller   fourchette   assiette   couteau   dessert

d légume   carafe   tasse   verre   soucoupe

e bière   melon   cidre   orangina   jus de fruit

2 Match the halves.

a une douzaine d'...   **i** ... vin rouge

b une carafe de ...   **ii** ... aux cerises

c une bouteille d' ...   **iii** ... escargots

d une tarte ...   **iv** ... crudités

e une assiette de ...   **v** ... orangina

3 Put these items in the right place on the menu.

tarte maison

service

moules

compris

hors-d'œuvre

> Potage
> ou
> **a** ....
> Steak-frites
> ou
> **b** ....
> Glace
> ou
> **c** ....
> 1/4 de vin rouge **d** ....
> **e** .... 15% non-compris

4 Find the French word which fits each of these definitions.

a Money you give the waiter for good service.

b A drink before the meal.

c The word used to summon a young female waitress.

d Describes a plain yoghurt.

e All kinds of things from the sea.

5 Fill in the gaps in this conversation at a restaurant.

> plat principal boisson bouteille pour commencer carte
> monsieur commander

CLIENT   Monsieur, la **a** .... s'il vous plaît.

GARÇON   Vous voulez **b** .... maintenant ?

CLIENT   **c** ...., je prends le potage.

GARÇON   Oui, **d** ....

CLIENT   Et comme **e** ...., je voudrais le steak.

GARÇON   Et comme **f** .... ?

CLIENT   Une **g** .... de vin rouge.

6 Solve the anagrams to find five snacks/fast-foods.

a zipaz   **b** brumharge   **c** wasncihd   **d** pêrce   **e** sacse-trocûe

7 Find six things you would see, but could not eat, in the restaurant.

A	D	D	I	T	I	O	N	R
C	M	K	E	F	B	C	H	V
A	O	U	R	B	O	L	R	E
R	C	U	I	L	L	E	R	R
A	Q	O	V	D	P	U	I	R
F	A	S	S	E	S	T	L	E
E	C	J	K	O	B	F	B	R
P	A	S	S	I	E	T	T	E

un adolescent	adolescent	fumer	to smoke
l'alcool	alcohol	grossir	to gain weight
*un athlète	athlete	s'habituer (à)	to get used to
le cancer	cancer	maigrir	to lose weight
le cœur	heart	menacer	to threaten
le danger	danger	mourir	to die
*le drogué	drug addict	persuader	to persuade
le fumeur	smoker	refuser	to refuse
le gosse	kid (child)	regretter	to regret
les jeunes (pl)	young people	risquer (de)	to risk
*les poumons (pl)	lungs	rouler	to travel/drive
*le régime	diet	savoir	to know
le risque	risk	suivre	to follow
le sport	sport		
le tabac	tobacco		
le taux (d'alcool)	(alcohol) level	au volant	at the (steering) wheel

la cigarette	cigarette	dangereux(euse)	dangerous
*la crise cardiaque	heart attack	en (bonne) forme	fit
*la drogue	drugs	*équilibré(e)	balanced
l'exercice	exercise	gros(se)	fat
la forme	fitness	important(e)	important
*les matières grasses (pl)	fats	*imprudent(e)	unwise
*la prévention routière	road safety	*inadmissible	unacceptable
		ivre	drunk
la réaction	reaction	lent(e)	slow
*la santé	health	malheureux(euse)	unhappy
		malheureusement	unfortunately
		pire	worse
conduire	to drive	trop	too (much)
se droguer	to take drugs		
éviter	to avoid		

1 Fill in the blanks in these sentences.

> dangereux   éviter   alcool   régime   refuser
> crise cardiaque   en forme   fumez

a Si vous ...., vous devez renoncer pour .... le cancer.

b Vous ne devez pas boire d'............ avant de conduire.

c Si vous mangez trop de matières grasses, vous risquez une ....

d L'alcool est .... au volant.

e Vous devez toujours .... la drogue.

f Pour rester ...., il est important d'avoir un .... équilibré.

2 Fill in the missing letters to find four positive words about healthy living.

a s _ _ _ é   **b** s _ _ _ t   **c** e _ _ _ _ _ _ e   **d** é _ _ _ _ _ _ _ é

3 Find the French word which fits each of these definitions.

a Personne qui fait beaucoup de sport.

b Personne qui a entre 10 et 16 ans.

c Personne qui a l'habitude de se droguer.

4 Find the opposites of these words.

a heureux   **b** acceptable   **c** prudent   **d** rapide   **e** sans risques

*le bâton de colle	glue stick	le (petit) job	(part-time) job
le boucher	butcher	le PDG (président-directeur-général)	managing director
le boulanger	baker	le journal	newspaper
le boulot	job (slang)	*le lecteur de disquettes	disk drive
le bureau	office	le logiciel	software
*le cédérom	CD-Rom	le maçon	builder
le chanteur	singer	le mannequin	model
*le chirurgien	surgeon	le mécanicien	mechanic
le classeur	file	le message	message
le clavier	keyboard	le métier	trade/job/craft
le client	customer	le minitel	computerised information system
le coiffeur	hairdresser		
le collègue	colleague		
le coup de téléphone	phone call		
le courrier (électronique)	mail (electronic)	*le mot de passe	password
le curseur	cursor	un ouvrier	worker
le directeur	manager	*un ouvrier agricole	farm worker
*le disque dur	hard disk	le patron	boss
un écran	screen	*le paysan	peasant
un électricien	electrician	*le projecteur	projector
un e-mail	e-mail	*le propriétaire	owner
un emploi	job	le répondeur	answering machine
un employé	employee/clerk	le salaire	salary
un employeur	employer	*le scotch	sellotape
*un expert consultant	consultant	le serveur	waiter
le fichier	filing cabinet	le stage	work experience
*le flic	cop, police officer	le traitement de texte	word-processing
un informaticien	computer scientist	le travail	work
		*le trombone	paperclip

le vendeur	salesman	taper (une lettre)	to type (a letter)
*le vigneron	vine cultivator	(taper à la machine)	(to do (some) typing)
une annonce	advert	*télécharger	to download
*la base de données	database	travailler	to work
la carrière	career	utiliser	to use
*la cartouche	cartridge (pen)		
la chanteuse	singer	Allô	Hello (on phone)
*la colle	glue		
la disquette	floppy disk	(un contrat) à durée déterminée	fixed-term (contract)
une équipe	team	à l'appareil	speaking (on the phone)
la fiche	form		
la formation	training	de bonne heure	early
une imprimante	printer	de la part de (qui?)	from (whom?)
*la perforeuse	hole punch	dur(e)	hard
*la puce	chip	essentiel(le)	essential
la réunion	meeting	fatigant(e)	tiring
une usine	factory	fatigué(e)	tired
		ne quittez pas	hold the line
*charger	to load	sans	without
choisir	to choose	varié(e)	varied
*classer	to file		
connaître	to know		
*copier	to copy		
*éditer	to edit		
*effacer	to delete		
faire des économies	to save up		
*fermer	to shut down		
*formater	to format		
imprimer	to print		
rappeler	to call back		

1 Find the odd word out in each of the following lists.

a fichier   coup de téléphone   collègue   e-mail   courrier

b imprimante   scotch   clavier   écran   curseur

c employé   patron   projecteur   propriétaire   employeur

d répondeur   réunion   classeur   trombone   colle

e client   maçon   vendeur   classeur   coiffeur

2 Complete this grid.

acteur	actrice
a	chanteuse
b	employée
c	ouvrière
d	paysanne
e	coiffeuse
f	directrice
g	informaticienne

3 Fill in the missing vowels to find five things you might use at work.

a d _ s q _ _ t t _   b p _ r f _ r _ _ s _   c f _ c h _   d c l _ v _ _ r
e l _ g _ c _ _ l

4 Find a French word to fit each of these definitions.

a Slang word for a job.

b The sort of learning you do at work.

c Place where people work to make things.

d You can't eat it, but a computer can't do without it.

e Sticky stuff.

f An expert brought in to solve problems.

5 Complete the crossword, and find another job.

a He sells things.

b She works for someone else.

c He operates on people.

d He keeps the law.

e He styles hair.

f He/She shows off clothes.

g He fixes computers.

6 Fill in the gaps in this telephone conversation.

quittez	rappeler	part	allô	directeur

SECRETAIRE	a ....
MADAME LEGRAND	Je voudrais parler au b ....
SECRETAIRE	C'est de la c .... de qui ?
MADAME LEGRAND	Madame Legrand.
SECRETAIRE	Ne d .... pas, madame. ... Je regrette, le directeur est absent. Il peut vous e .... ?

7 Solve the anagrams to find four words connected with computers.

a equsid   b cepu   c mefortar   d cétherléarg

T h e   W o r l d   o f   W o r k   73

*l'alpinisme	mountaineering	le rendez-vous	date
*les arts martiaux	martial arts	le roman	novel
l'athlétisme	athletics	le rugby	rugby
le bal	dance	le ski (nautique)	(water) skiing
*le baladeur	personal stereo	*le spectateur	spectator
		le stade	stadium/ground
le ballon	ball	le tennis	tennis
le CD	CD	(de table)	(table-tennis)
le centre sportif	sports/leisure centre	le terrain	pitch
		*le tournoi	competition
le complexe sportif	sports/leisure centre	le violon	violin
		le volley	volleyball
*le compositeur	composer	*le VTT	mountain bike
le court de tennis	tennis court	le zoo	zoo
le cyclisme	cycling		
le disque (compact)	record (compact disc)	*une ambiance	atmosphere
les échecs (pl)	chess	la bande dessinée	cartoon
le foot(ball)	football	la batterie	drums
le groupe	group	la boîte (de nuit)	(night) club
le handball	handball	les boules (pl)	(French) bowls
le hockey	hockey	la canne à pêche	fishing rod
le jeu (vidéo)	(video) game	les cartes (pl)	cards
le jeu de société	board game	la danse	dancing
le jeu électronique	computer game	*la détente	relaxation
		la discothèque	disco
*le joueur	player	*les distractions	entertainment
le loisir	leisure	une équipe	team
le match	match	l'équitation	horse-riding
le passe-temps	hobby/pastime	*la fête foraine	funfair
le patinage	skating	la flûte (à bec)	flute (recorder)
le patin (à roulettes/ sur glace)	(roller/ice) skating	la guitare	guitar
le piano	piano	la lecture	reading

la Maison des Jeunes (la MJC)	Youth Club	(faire du sport)	(to do sport)
		(faire du vélo)	(to go cycling)
la musique (pop/classique/rock)	(pop/classical/rock) music	faire partie de	to belong to
		*faire une partie de	to have a game of
la natation	swimming		
la partie (de)	game (of)	s'intéresser	to be interested in
la patinoire	skating rink		
la pêche	fishing	jouer à	to play (+ sport/game)
la photographie	photography		
la piscine	swimming baths	(jouer au tennis)	(to play tennis)
		jouer de	to play (+ instrument)
la planche (à voile) (à roulettes)	windsurfing (skate-boarding)		
		(jouer de la batterie)	(to play the drums)
la promenade (à vélo/en bateau)	walk(ing) (bike/boat ride)	lire	to read
		monter	to climb
*la randonnée	rambling	montrer	to show
la trompette	trumpet	nager	to swim
la voile	sailing	s'occuper de	to see to
		plonger	to dive
aller à la pêche	to go fishing	se promener	to go for a walk
s'amuser	to enjoy oneself	regarder	to watch
		rentrer	to go home
chanter	to sing	sembler	to seem
*chanter dans la chorale	to sing in a choir	sortir	to go out
		surfer sur internet	to surf the net
danser	to dance		
*se détendre	to relax	fana(tique)	fan(atical)
écouter	to listen (to)	favori(te)	favourite
*s'entraîner	to train	*match nul	draw
faire (+ activities not played)	to go, do	passionnant(e)	exciting
		sensass	brilliant
(faire du patin)	(to go skating)	sportif(ive)	sporty
(faire du cheval)	(to go horse riding)		

1 Find the French game/sport which fits these definitions.

a Style of combat which came from the East.

b Played on a board with 64 squares.

c A cross between basketball and 5-a-side football.

d You play with 52 of these.

e Often played on the beach – even in the Olympics!

2 Find six musical instruments in this wordsearch.

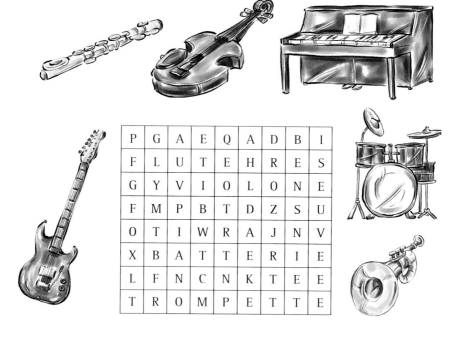

P	G	A	E	Q	A	D	B	I
F	L	U	T	E	H	R	E	S
G	Y	V	I	O	L	O	N	E
F	M	P	B	T	D	Z	S	U
O	T	I	W	R	A	J	N	V
X	B	A	T	T	E	R	I	E
L	F	N	C	N	K	T	E	E
T	R	O	M	P	E	T	T	E

3 Fill in the missing letters to find five leisure activities.

a l _ _ _ _ r e

b _ _ p i n i _ _ _

c v _ _ _ e

d c _ _ _ _ _ m e

e p _ _ _ _ n _ _ e

Complete the following sentences with an appropriate adjective.

a Je suis .... de rugby.

b Le football, c'est vraiment .... !

c Mon sport ...., c'est le tennis.

d L'équitation est ....

e Je ne suis pas très ....

5 Which is the odd word out in each of the following lists?

a patin à roulettes   ski nautique   planche à voile   natation   voile

b danse   discothèque   guitare   piscine   musique

c cyclisme   bande dessinée   VTT   ski nautique   équitation

d stade   passe-temps   MJC   complexe sportif   terrain

6 Complete the following sentences with the appropriate verb.

écouter   danser   s'entraîner   lire   nager

a Elle va .... pour le match de tennis.

b J'adore .... à la piscine.

c Je préfère .... mes CD.

d J'aime ....des romans.

e Ce soir, je vais .... dans une boîte de nuit.

7 Solve the following clues.

a On pratique ce sport à cheval.

b On pratique ce sport en montagne.

c Un concours entre deux équipes.

d Stade spécial où on fait du patin à glace.

*un abonnement	subscription
un acteur	actor
*un animateur	presenter
un article	article
le balcon	balcony
*le casque	headset
le cinéma	cinema
*le courrier du cœur	agony column
le dessin animé	cartoon (film)
le documentaire	documentary
*le drame	drama
un écran	screen
le feuilleton	soap/serial
le film	film
(comique)	(comedy)
(d'amour)	(love story)
(d'aventures)	(adventure)
(d'épouvante)	(horror)
(d'horreur)	(horror)
(de science fiction)	(science fiction)
(policier)	(crime)
(western)	(cowboy)
le flash (d'information) (-info)	news flash
*FR3	French TV channel
le jeu télévisé	game show
le journal	newspaper
le journaliste	journalist
*le lecteur	reader
le magazine	magazine

l'orchestre	stalls (downstairs seats)
le présentateur	presenter
*le quotidien	daily paper
*le reportage	press report
le sous-titre	sub-title
le spectacle	show
le téléfilm	TV film
le téléspectateur	viewer
le télétel	teletext
le théâtre	theatre
le tube	hit record
le (gros) titre	headline

les actualités	current affairs
*une antenne (parabolique)	aerial (satellite dish)
la caméra	(film/tv camera)
la chaîne	channel
la comédie	comedy
une émission (de sport)	(sports) programme
une image	picture
les informations (pl) (les infos)	news
la page	page
la parole	word
*la photo satellite	satellite picture
la pièce (de théâtre)	play
la place	seat
la presse	press

la publicité (la pub)	advert/ advertising	se rappeler	to recall
la radio	radio	rire	to laugh
la revue	(glossy) magazine	*tourner un film	to make a film
la salle (cinéma à 5 salles)	auditorium (5-screen cinema)	amusant(e)	amusing
*la scène	stage	drôle	funny
la séance	performance/ show	en couleur	in colour
la série	series	en noir et blanc	in black and white
la télévision (par satellite) (*par câble)	television (satellite) (cable)	il s'agit de...	it's about ...
		libre (radio libre)	independent (independent radio)
la tournée	tour (of singer etc)	plusieurs	several
*la tragédie	tragedy	recherché(e)	obscure
la vedette	(film) star	romantique	romantic
la version (française) (originale)	(French) version/ soundtrack (original soundtrack)	sous-titré(e)	sub-titled

*s'amuser	to have a good time
avoir peur	to be frightened
commencer	to start
effrayer	to frighten
faire peur à	to frighten
passer à (la radio/la télé)	to be on (radio/TV)
plaire (le film m'a plu)	to please (I liked the film)

20 Media (cinema, television, theatre)

1 Put these words into the appropriate column.

scène   film d'épouvante   informations   pièce   balcon
chaîne   feuilleton   séance

Télévision	Théâtre

2 Find the odd word out in each of these lists.

a amour   vedette   horreur   aventures   épouvante

b lecteur   satellite   FR3   antenne   câblé

c policier   courrier du cœur   comique   aventures   horreur

d image   lecteur   rédacteur   journaliste   présentateur

e journal   caméra   magazine   revue   presse

3 Complete the following sentences.

amour   amusantes   épouvante   en noir et blanc   comiques

a J'aime bien les films d'.................. . Ils me font peur.

b J'aime les films .... Je les trouve drôles.

c Je n'aime pas les films d'............. . Ils sont trop romantiques.

d J'aime les comédies. Elles sont ....

e Je n'aime pas les vieux films. Ils sont ....

4 Solve the anagrams to find five words to do with broadcasting.

a simiéons   b ementocairdu   c clubpitéi   d éries   e înecha

5 Find a French word/phrase to fit each of these definitions.

a Letters to a magazine talking about problems.

b Members of the public appear in this to win prizes.

c The most important actor in a film.

d Series of drawings which give a moving picture.

e Newspapers, magazines, radio, television etc.

6 Find seven different types of film in this wordsearch.

C	D	F	P	R	L	W	N	E	S
P	H	A	G	F	E	E	T	P	C
A	O	C	M	L	E	S	R	O	O
B	R	L	N	O	S	T	P	U	M
X	R	V	I	T	U	E	L	V	I
Q	E	N	E	C	T	R	M	A	Q
M	U	F	Y	S	I	N	Q	N	U
N	R	P	T	L	V	E	R	T	E
C	A	V	E	N	T	U	R	E	S

7 Fill in the missing letters to find five words to do with the cinema.

a s _ _ _ e   c é _ _ _ n   e v _ _ _ _ _ e

b s _ _ _ _ e   d s _ _ _ - _ _ _ _ e

l'amour	love	admirer	to admire
le bijou	jewel	appeler	to call
*le but	goal	se comporter	to behave
le caractère	personality	se disputer	to argue
le champion	champion	s'entendre (avec)	to get on (with)
le championnat	championship	espérer	to hope
le chanteur	singer	*se fâcher	to get angry
le footballeur	footballer	gagner	to win
*le héros	hero	*marquer (un but)	to score (a goal)
un homme	man	pleurer	to cry
*le joueur (de rugby)	(rugby) player	réussir	to succeed
le peintre	painter	se taire	to be silent
le petit ami	boyfriend		
le piercing	(body) piercing	*absolument	absolutely
les rapports (pl)	relationship(s)	aimable	likeable
*le sens de l'humour	sense of humour	amoureux(euse) (de)	in love (with)
*le teint	complexion	amusant(e)	funny
les vêtements (pl)	clothes	au début	at the beginning
le visage	face	*bavard(e)	chatty
		beau (belle)	handsome
la bêtise	something stupid	bête	silly
la chance	luck	bien	well
la date (de naissance)	(birth) date	bizarre	odd/strange
la femme	woman	blond(e)	blond
*la frange	fringe	célèbre	famous
l'héroïne	heroine	célibataire	unmarried
la permission	permission	charmant(e)	charming
la petite amie	girlfriend	chouette	terrific
*la queue de cheval	ponytail	comme	like
		*consciencieux(euse)	conscientious

courageux(euse)	brave
cruel(le)	cruel
*de bonne humeur	in a good mood
*de mauvaise humeur	in a bad mood
dernier(ière)	latest
*distrait(e)	absent-minded
dynamique	energetic
égoïste	selfish
élégant(e)	elegant
embêtant(e)	annoying
en colère	angry
excellent(e)	excellent
fâché(e)	angry
faible	weak
généreux(euse)	generous
*génial(e)	brilliant
habillé(e)	dressed
heureux(euse)	happy
honnête	honest
idiot(e)	daft
impoli(e)	impolite
impressionnant(e)	impressive
intelligent(e)	intelligent
jaloux(ouse)	jealous
jeune	young
joli(e)	pretty
laid(e)	ugly
maigre	thin
malgré	in spite of
méchant(e)	nasty

merveilleux(euse)	marvellous
mince	slim
méchant(e)	nasty
moche	bad, not cool
mûr(e)	mature
né(e)	born
ouvert(e)	outgoing
paresseux(euse)	lazy
pénible	tiresome
pessimiste	pessimistic
poli(e)	polite
sage	well-behaved
silencieux(euse)	silent
stupide	stupid
sympa(thique)	nice
timide	shy/timid
tout le monde	everybody
*travailleur(euse)	hard-working
triste	sad

1 Put each of these adjectives into the appropriate column.

aimable   cruel   méchant   stupide   généreux

génial   égoïste   charmant   paresseux   consciencieux

Positif	Négatif

2 Complete the crossword, and find another word to describe each person.

a This person is looked up to by others.

b This person takes part in a game.

c This person is the best of the lot.

d This is a female person.

e This person paints pictures.

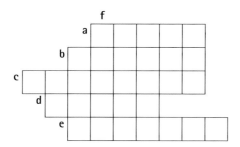

3 Fill in the blanks in these sentences with the appropriate verb.

espère   fâchent   disputé   s'entendent   marqué   gagné

a Je me suis .... avec ma petite amie.

b Mon footballeur préféré a .... le championnat trois fois.

c Il a .... beaucoup de buts.

d J' .... parler avec mon héros.

e Mes parents .... bien avec mes amies.

f Ils se .... au sujet de mes piercings.

4 Find the opposite of each of these words.

a courageux   **b** stupide   **c** impoli   **d** de mauvaise humeur   **e** joli

5 Find a French word to match each of these descriptions.

a Someone who talks a lot.

b The ability to find things funny.

c What someone wears.

d The day someone is born.

e Hair that is tied back and hanging down.

6 Solve the anagrams to find five things you might like about someone.

a olip   **b** thimpaysequ   **c** quimandye   **d** iblamea   **e** hontêne

7 Now fill in the missing letters to find five qualities you might not like about them.

a j _ _ _ _ x   **c** c _ _ _ l   **e** b _ _ _ _ _ e

b p _ _ _ _ _ e   **d** é _ _ _ _ _ e

un échange	exchange
le lendemain	next day
le matin	morning

une invitation	invitation
la rencontre	meeting
la visite	visit

accepter	to accept
accompagner	to accompany
accueillir	to welcome
aller chercher	to fetch/ collect
amener	to bring (someone)
apporter	to bring (something)
s'asseoir	to sit down
décider	to decide
*donner rendez-vous	to arrange to meet
embrasser	to kiss
être en train de ...	to be busy doing ...
être sur le point de ...	to be on the point of ...
faire la connaissance	to make the acquaintance
inviter	to invite
manquer (le bus)	to miss (the bus)
proposer	to suggest
remercier	to thank

rencontrer	to meet (for the first time, or by chance)
rendre visite à	to visit
retrouver	to meet
saluer	to greet
tutoyer	to call someone 'tu'
venir	to come
*venir chercher	to come and call for

A bientôt!	See you soon!
A demain!	See you tomorrow!
A tout à l'heure!	See you later!
Au revoir!	Goodbye!
Bienvenue!	Welcome!
Bonjour!	Hello/Good morning!
Bon séjour!	Have a nice stay!
Bonsoir!	Good evening!
Bonne chance!	Good luck!
Bonne nuit!	Good night!
Désolé(e)!	Sorry!

lundi	Mon	vendredi	Fri
mardi	Tue	samedi	Sat
mercredi	Wed	dimanche	Sun
jeudi	Thurs		

Enchanté(e)!	Pleased to meet you!
Entendu!	Agreed!

Salut!	Hi!	Ça va?	Are you OK?
après-demain	the day after tomorrow	Ça va	I'm OK
		certainement	certainly
aujourd'hui	today	d'abord	first
*avant-hier	the day before yesterday	d'accord	OK/All right
		dans	in
ce matin	this morning	dans (dix) minutes	in (ten) minutes
cet après-midi	this afternoon	de rien	don't mention it
ce soir	tonight	en avance	early
demain	tomorrow	là	there
hier	yesterday	là-bas	over there

				madame	Madam/Mrs/Ms
janvier	Jan	juillet	July	mademoiselle	Miss
février	Feb	août	Aug	maintenant	now
mars	Mar	septembre	Sept	malheureusement	unfortunately
avril	Apr	octobre	Oct	merci (pour)	thank you (for)
mai	May	novembre	Nov	midi	midday
juin	Jun	décembre	Dec	monsieur	Sir/Mr

au mois de (mai)	in the month of (May)	occupé(e)	busy
en (janvier)	in (January)	pardon	sorry
à l'heure	on time	prière de	please
à part	apart from	ravi(e)	delighted
au bout de (la rue)	at the end of (the street)	Asseyez-vous! (Assieds-toi!)	Sit down!
au coin (de)	at the corner (of)	Entre(z)!	Come in!
au milieu (de)	in the middle (of)	(... à quelle heure?)	(What time?)
avec plaisir	with pleasure	Si on allait ...	How about going ...
bien entendu	of course	Voici (Marie)	Here is/This is (Marie)
bien sûr	of course		
bientôt	soon		

1 Find the odd word out in each of the following lists.

a dimanche   août   mardi   mercredi   samedi

b automne   printemps   aujourd'hui   hiver   été

c soir   juillet   mars   juin   février

d accueillir   rencontrer   désolé   faire la connaissance   embrasser

e Bonjour   Bonsoir   Au revoir   Enchanté   Salut

f A demain   Bienvenue   Bonne nuit   A tout à l'heure   A bientôt

2 Find a French word or phrase to fit each of these definitions.

a To arrange an appointment to see someone.

b To call someone 'tu'.

c To be on the point of ...

d To go to someone's house to pick them up.

e To fail to catch (e.g. a train).

3 Complete the following sentences with the appropriate verb.

embrassée   proposé   décidé   remercié   accepter

a Je veux bien .... votre invitation.

b Il a .... de venir me chercher.

c Il m'a .... et il a dit « Bon voyage ! »

d Mon correspondant m'a .... un échange.

e Je l'ai .... de son hospitalité.

4 Complete these phrases. (They're all about time.)

a à l'_ _ _ _ _   **d** c _   m _ _ _ _

b d _ _ _   cinq   m _ _ _ _ _ s   **e** le l _ _ _ _ _ _ _ n

c à q _ _ _ _ _   h _ _ _ _ ?

5 If this is maintenant

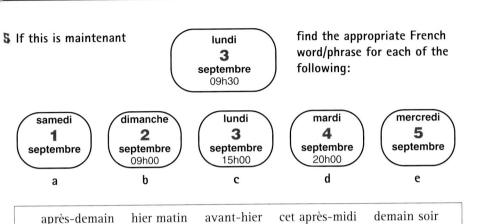

find the appropriate French word/phrase for each of the following:

lundi **3** septembre 09h30	

samedi **1** septembre
a

dimanche **2** septembre 09h00
b

lundi **3** septembre 15h00
c

mardi **4** septembre 20h00
d

mercredi **5** septembre
e

après-demain   hier matin   avant-hier   cet après-midi   demain soir

6 Solve the clues to find the French for six words you might use when accepting an invitation.

a certainly   **b** see you soon   **c** with pleasure   **d** OK   **e** delighted

f

a

b

c

d

e

7 Fill in the gaps in the following telephone conversation.

demain   viendrai te chercher   merci   bien sûr   salut   à demain

THOMAS   Allô, ici Thomas.

SOPHIE   **a**............., Thomas.

THOMAS   Tu vas à la boum chez Marc **b**............... soir ?

SOPHIE   Oui **c**......................... .

THOMAS   Alors, je **d**.................... à huit heures. **e**................. .

SOPHIE   D'accord. **f**............... Thomas.

les achats (pl)	shopping/ purchases	la bijouterie	jeweller's
un appareil photo	camera	la boîte	tin
un ascenseur	lift	la boucherie	butcher's
le bricolage	Do-It-Yourself	la boulangerie	baker's
*le caméscope	camcorder	*la carte bleue	major French credit card
le centre commercial	shopping centre	la casserole	saucepan
le choix	choice	la charcuterie	cooked meat shop
*un escalier roulant	escalator	la confiserie	sweet shop
*le grand magasin	department store	*les conserves (pl)	tinned foods
un hypermarché	hypermarket	une dizaine	(about) ten
le jeu (de société)	(board) game	la douzaine	dozen
le jouet	toy	une enveloppe	envelope
le kiosque à journaux	news stand	une épicerie	grocer's
le marchand	shopkeeper/ stallholder	la fermeture (annuelle)	(annual) closing
le marché	market	la fin	end
le mètre	metre	la grande surface	supermarket/ hypermarket
le morceau	piece	la librairie	bookshop
le prix	price	la monnaie	change
le rayon (boucherie)	(butchery) department	l'ouverture	opening
*le reçu	receipt	la papeterie	stationer's
le self	self-service restaurant	la parfumerie	perfume shop
		la pâtisserie	cake shop
les soldes (pl)	sales	la pharmacie	chemist's
le sous-sol	basement	la poissonnerie	fish shop
le supermarché	supermarket	la promotion	special offer
le (bureau de) tabac	tobacconist's	*les provisions	groceries
		*la quincaillerie	hardware shop

la réduction	reduction	d'occasion	secondhand
la vitrine	shop-window	d'une grande valeur	expensive
la TVA	VAT	en bois	(made of) wood
		en métal	(made of) metal
acheter	to buy	en plastique	(made of) plastic
commander	to order		
coûter	to cost	*entrée libre	browsers welcome
demander	to ask for		
dépenser	to spend	exceptionnel(le)	exceptional
échanger	to exchange	frais (fraîche)	fresh
faire du lèche-vitrine	to go window-shopping	... grammes de	... grams of
		gratuit(e)	free
		interdit(e)	forbidden
*faire un paquet-cadeau	to wrap up as a gift	Je peux vous aider?	Can I help you?
payer	to pay (for)	Je le/la/les prends.	I'll take it/them.
*se plaindre	to complain	Je voudrais ...	I'd like ...
pousser	to push	Je vous en prie.	It's my pleasure.
rembourser	to reimburse		
tirer	to pull	léger(ère)	light
*valoir	to be worth	neuf (neuve)	new
vendre	to sell	nouveau (nouvelle)	new
		(dix) pour cent	(ten) per cent
affreux(euse)	horrible	(3) pour le prix de (2)	(3) for the price of (2)
bon marché	cheap	réduit(e)	reduced
cher (chère)	dear/expensive	satisfait(e)	satisfied
combien	how many/ how much	surgelé(e)	frozen
		un kilo de	a kilo of
C'est combien?	How much is it?	un litre de	a litre of
		un paquet de	a packet of
Défense de (fumer)	No (smoking)		
disponible	available		

1 Which is the correct word?

a Pour acheter du parfum je vais à la parfumerie/poissonnerie.

b Est-ce que vous pouvez me faire du lèche-vitrine/faire un paquet-cadeau?

c Pour aller au sous-sol je prends l'ascenseur/l'appareil photo.

d Est-ce qu'il y a un kiosque à journaux/une vitrine près d'ici?

e J'ai payé/coûté mes achats.

2 Match the halves.

a un kilo de ...   i   ... jambon

b un litre de ...   ii   ... plastique

c un paquet de ...   iii ... carottes

d 200 grammes de ...   iv   ... chips

e un jouet en ...   v   ... vin rouge

3 Complete the crossword with six names of shops – and find another place to buy things.

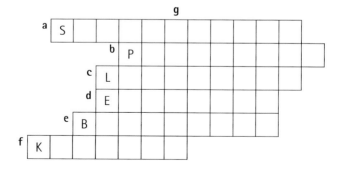

4 Fill in the missing letters to find five non-food items.

a _ _ s s _ _ _ l e   c j _ _ _ _ s _ c _ _ t _   e _ n v _ l _ p p _

b c _ m _ s c _ p _   d _ p p _ r _ _ l p h _ t _

5 Find a French word to fit each of these definitions.

a Where you go to buy a necklace.

b To make into an attractive parcel.

c Period when the shopkeeper is away for his yearly holiday.

d Twelve items.

e Not at all cheap.

6 Complete the following announcements which you might hear in a supermarket.

> promotion   achetez   réduction   gratuit   pour le prix de deux

a .... de quinze pour cent au rayon librairie.

b Trois CD ....

c .... sur tous les jouets.

d .... trois porte-clés, recevez un quatrième e ....

7 Solve the anagrams to find five ways of describing goods.

a faruxef   b duirét   c chefaîr   d uonevua   e onb craméh

un anorak	anorak	le pull-(over)	sweater/ pullover
les bas (pl)	stockings	le rouge à lèvres	lipstick
le blouson	(short) jacket	le short	shorts
le bonnet	woolly hat	le slip	underpants
le bouton	button	(de bain)	(swimming
le chapeau	hat		trunks)
le chausson	slipper	le soutien-gorge	bra
le chemisier	blouse	le survêtement	tracksuit
le collant	tights	le sweat-shirt	sweat shirt
le corsage	blouse	le T-shirt	T-shirt
le costume	suit	le tricot	jumper
le coton	cotton	les vêtements (pl)	clothes
le foulard	scarf		
les gants (pl)	gloves	les baskets (pl)	trainers
le gant de toilette	flannel	les bottes (pl)	boots
le gilet	waistcoat, cardigan	la casquette	cap
		la ceinture	belt
un imperméable (un imper)	mac/raincoat	les chaussettes (pl)	socks
		les chaussures (pl)	shoes
le jean	jeans	la chemise	shirt
le jogging	tracksuit	*la chemise de nuit	nightie
*le lavage à la main	hand-washing	la cravate	tie
le look	image/fashion	la culotte	panties
le maillot (de bain)	swimming costume	une écharpe	scarf
		*la fermeture éclair	zip-fastener
le manteau	coat	*la gamme	range
le mouchoir	handkerchief	la jupe	skirt
*le nettoyage à sec	dry-cleaning	la laine	wool
le nylon	nylon	la mode	fashion
le pantalon	trousers	la paire	pair
le pardessus	overcoat	la pointure	size (of shoes)
le parfum	perfume		

*la revue de mode	fashion magazine	Ça me va?	Does it suit me?
la robe	dress	Ça ne me va pas.	It doesn't suit me.
la robe de chambre	dressing gown	court(e)	short
les sandales (pl)	sandals	déchiré(e)	torn
la taille	size (of clothes)	de marque	branded
la veste	jacket	dépassé(e)	out of date
		en coton	in cotton
essayer	to try (on)	en (laine)	in (wool)
manquer (il manque un bouton)	to lack (there's a button missing)	en (noir)	in (black)
		en (trente-neuf)	in (size 39)
		*étroit(e)	narrow
mettre	to put on	*griffé(e)	designer
porter	to wear	long(ue)	long
*rétrécir	to shrink	lourd(e)	heavy
		Quelle pointure?	What size? (for shoes)
blanc (blanche)	white	Quelle taille?	What size? (for clothes)
bleu(e)	blue		
brun(e)	brown	rayé(e)	striped
gris(e)	grey	serré(e)	tight
jaune	yellow	uni(e)	plain/self-coloured
marron	brown		
noir(e)	black	vêtu(e)	dressed
rose	pink		
rouge	red		
vert(e)	green		
violet(te)	violet		
(bleu) clair	light (blue)		
(vert) foncé	dark (green)		
(rouge) vif	bright (red)		
à carreaux	checked		

1 Find the odd word out in the following lists.

a slip   culotte   veste   soutien-gorge   sous-vêtements

b chaussures   baskets   sandales   bottes   chapeau

c jupe   robe   pardessus   collant   chemisier

d maillot de bain   anorak   écharpe   gants   manteau

e survêtement   chemise de nuit   jogging   baskets   short

2 Fill in the missing vowels to find five words/phrases you might find on a clothes label.

a l _ v _ g _ _ l _ m _ _ n   d c _ t _ n

b l _ _ n _   e t _ _ l l _

c n _ t t _ y _ g _ _ s _ c

3 Find nine colours in this wordsearch.

G	V	E	R	T	P	Q	Y	R
V	R	I	R	O	U	G	E	J
C	A	I	O	B	R	U	N	A
E	S	W	S	L	B	L	E	U
R	U	D	E	A	E	W	I	N
T	O	Q	C	N	P	T	X	E
I	N	U	J	C	A	E	E	B

4 Find a French word to fit each of these definitions.

a Matching jacket and trousers.

b You wear it when it's raining.

c Everything you wear.

d Alternative to buttons.

e It holds your trousers up.

5 Solve the anagrams to find five words used to describe clothes.

   a rerés   **b** ungole   **c** éyear   **d** trocu   **e** torité

6 Complete the crossword to find six items of cold-weather clothing, and discover another one.

		g					
a		L	O			O	
b		R		K			
c		N	T				
d		N		E			
e	C	H		P			
f		R			S		S

*le cambriolage	burglary	*le réfugié	refugee
*le cambrioleur	burglar	*le sida	aids
le changement	change	*le stress	stress
les chiffres (pl)	figures	*un SDF	homeless
le ciel	sky	(sans domicile fixe)	person
le climat	climate	*le tabagisme	smoking
le coup de soleil	sunburn	*le tiers-monde	third world
le crime	crime	*le tremblement	earthquake
*le dauphin	dolphin	de terre	
*les déchets (pl)	waste	*le vol	theft
le détritus	rubbish	*le vol à l'étalage	shoplifting
*un éboulement	collapse	*le voleur	thief
*l'effet de serre	greenhouse effect	*le voyou	hooligan
*l'électricité	electricity	*une amélioration	improvement
un embouteillage	traffic jam	*la bataille	battle
*l'environnement	environment	*la centrale	nuclear power
l'espace	space	nucléaire	station
le gaz	gas	la circulation	traffic
*les gaz (pl) d'échappement	exhaust gases	la cité	(housing) estate
*un immigré	immigrant	la conservation	conservation
le logement	housing	*la couche d'ozone	ozone layer
*le manque de pluie	lack of rain	la destruction	destruction
le monde	the world	l'énergie	energy
*l'occident	the West	la faim	hunger
*l'orient	the East	*la forêt tropicale	tropical forest
*les pays développés	developed countries	*la fuite	leak
*les pays en voie de développement	developing countries	*la fumée	smoke
		*une inondation	flood
*le préjugé	prejudice	la lumière	light
*le recyclage des déchets	recycling of waste	la maladie	illness
		*la manifestation	demonstration
		*la marée noire	oil slick

*les ordures ménagères	household refuse	*se réfugier	to seek asylum
*la politique	politics	*respirer	to breathe
la pollution	pollution	sauver	to save
la raison	reason	*tuer	to kill
*les ressources (pl)	resources		
*la sécheresse	drought	à cause de	because of
*la société	society	à peu près	nearly
la source	source	*affreux(euse)	awful
la terre	earth	ainsi	in this way
*la vague	wave	*assez (de)	enough (of)
*la violence	violence	atmosphérique	atmospheric
la vitesse	speed	autre	other
		biodégradable	biodegradable
arrêter	to stop	*chimique	chemical
avoir besoin (de)	to need	compliqué(e)	complicated
avoir faim	to be hungry	en voie de disparition	endangered
*avoir raison	to be right		
*avoir tort	to be wrong	épuisé(e)	exhausted
*se battre	to beat	naturel(le)	natural
*cambrioler	to burgle	nécessaire	necessary
causer	to cause	nucléaire	nuclear
comprendre	to understand	*occidental(e)	Western
conserver	to preserve	*oriental(e)	Eastern
*détruire	to destroy	par terre	on the ground
*s'échapper	to escape	pollué(e)	polluted
épuiser	to exhaust, use up	renouvelable	renewable
		*sans abri	homeless
*essayer une drogue	to try a drug	*sans domicile fixe (SDF)	homeless
*gaspiller	to waste		
jeter	to throw away	solaire	solar
*polluer	to pollute	vite	fast/quickly
recycler	to recycle		

1 Find a French word to match each of these definitions.

a One who breaks in and steals.

b Not having enough to eat.

c Person who has nowhere to live.

d The poorest parts of the planet.

e Dry period.

2 Find the odd word out in each of these lists.

a voleur   voyou   dauphin   cambrioleur   SDF

b embouteillage   coup de soleil   allergie   maladie   sida

c violence   cambriolage   vol   amélioration   vol à l'étalage

d pollution   vitesse   gaz d'échappement   circulation   coup de soleil

e gaspiller   détruire   recycler   polluer   tuer

3 Choose the correct word or phrase.

a Les pays développés/les pays en voie de développement sont les pays les plus riches.

b Le tabagisme/la sécheresse est un problème dans les pays de l'occident.

c Il ne faut pas polluer/recycler des océans.

d Le manque de pluie/le manque de circulation est un grand problème dans le tiers-monde.

e Parmi les SDF il y a des réfugiés/dauphins.

4 Fill in the missing letters to find five 'green' words.

a r _ c y c l _ g _   c c _ _ c h _ d' _ z _ n _   e _ r d _ r _ s

b p _ l l _ _ r   d _ n v _ r _ n n _ m _ n t

5 Find the opposite of each of these words/phrases.

a avoir raison   b conserver   c orient   d danger   e pays développé

6 Solve the anagrams to find five words to do with social problems.

a nass riab   b gedruo   c mibagaste   d fugiéér

7 Which of the following are thought to be due to exhaust fumes?

a l'effet de serre

b le vol à l'étalage

c le tabagisme

d la marée noire

e la destruction de la couche d'ozone

f les SDF

g le cambriolage

h l'amélioration des forêts tropicales

i le changement du climat

Time

bientôt	soon
de nouveau	again
déjà	already
dernier(ière)	last
encore (une fois)	(once) again
enfin	at last
ensuite	then
environ	about
longtemps	for a long time
lorsque	when
parfois	sometimes
pendant	during
(plus) tard	late(r)
prochain(e)	next
puis	then
quelquefois	sometimes
récemment	recently
soudain	suddenly
tôt	early
*tout de suite	immediately

Place

au-dessous (de)	below
au-dessus (de)	above
arrière	back/rear
chez	at the house of
derrière	behind
devant	in front
en bas	at the bottom/ downstairs
en haut	at the top/ upstairs
ensemble	together
ici	here
là-bas	(over) there
là-haut	up there
parmi	amongst
partout	everywhere
sous	under
sur	on
toutes directions	all routes
est	east
nord	north
ouest	west
sud	south

Argument

à moi	mine
à mon avis	in my opinion
alors	then
autre	other
un avantage	advantage
bref	in brief
car	for/because
contre	against
d'abord	firstly
donc	so/therefore

faux(sse)	false
impossible	impossible
un inconvénient	disadvantage
mais	but
nécessaire	necessary
obligatoire	compulsory
parce que	because
par exemple	for example
peut-être	perhaps
plutôt	rather
possible	possible
pour	for/in order to
pourtant	however
pourquoi	why
le problème	problem
quand même	even so
selon	according to
surtout	above all
tout à fait	completely
vrai(e)	true

Negation

ne ... aucun	not any
ne ... jamais	never
ne ... ni ... ni	neither ... nor
ne ... pas	not
ne ... personne	nobody/no-one
ne ... plus	no more/no longer

| ne ... que | only |
| ne ... rien | nothing |

Quantity/degree

aussi	also
la moitié	half
pareil(le)	similar/same
peu	little
la plupart (de)	most (of)
plus (que)	more (than)
presque	almost
sauf	except
seulement	only
tant	so much

comparer	to compare
croire	to think
se débrouiller	to sort oneself out
se dépêcher	to hurry
désirer	to want
dire	to say
s'écrire	to be written
parler	to speak
penser	to think
raconter	to tell (a story)
sourire	to smile
terminer	to finish
voir	to see
vouloir	to want

1 Self, Family & Friends

1 a oncle b neveu c femme
  d mari e fils

2 a ouvrier b naissance
  c célibataire d poisson
  e animal

3 a tante b oncle b grand-père
  d frère e nièce

4 a grands-parents b frères
  c animaux d travaille
  e parents

5 a copain - friend
  b correspondant - penfriend
  c prénom - first name
  d meilleur - best
  e lunettes - glasses

6 Animal: le chat, le cheval, le lapin
  le poisson rouge, la souris.

  Travail: un agent de police,
  le caissier, le chauffeur, le facteur
  l'employée de bureau.

  Famille: la demi-sœur, la nièce,
  le demi-frère, le mari, la tante.

7 a cheval b cobaye c poisson
  d souris e chien f lapin

8 bonjour appelle ans
  anniversaire sœur yeux
  cheveux frère appelle
  mignon

2 Local area and weather

1 a le bâtiment b le centre-ville
  c le soleil d le trajet

2 a collège b place c une fontaine
  d des nuages

3 le métro la gare routière
  le musée le bâtiment
  le grand magasin la place
  la zone piétonne le jardin public

4 a brouillard b neige c mauvais
  d pleut

5 a vieille b bruyant c industrielle
  d historique e vieux

6 Magasins: le marché la boutique
  Chemin de fer: le train la gare
  le trajet
  La ville: le château le musée
  le jardin zoologique

7 ville piétonne boutiques
  magasins touristes musées
  cathédrale magnifique mer

8 a le château le collège
  la cathédrale b refer to page 11
  c un arbre le champ le paysage
  la colline la ferme

3 School life

1 a chimie b français c informatique
  d histoire e EPS f maths

2 **a** dessin **b** enseignement
c faute **d** cartable **e** devoirs

3 trousse taille-crayon règle
calculatrice gomme crayon

4 **a** neuf heures **b** une heure
c 10 minutes **d** 15h30

5 magnétophone tableau papier

6 Positif : fort sympa intéressant
Négatif : retenue difficile nul
sévère ennuyeux

7 **a** bavarder **b** dessine **c** passe
d prêter

4 Education, careers and future plans

1 **a** apprenti **b** mécanicien
c client **d** patron
e comptable

2 **a** mal payé **b** boucle d'oreille

3 Positif : bien qualifié
bien payé sûr

Négatif : chômage violence
démodé

4 **a** une licence **b** un stagiaire
c la médecine **d** le tourisme
e mes études

5 **a** continuer **b** rencontrer
c perfectionner **d** envoyer
e gagner

6 **a** le maquillage **b** les bijoux
c le vandalisme

7 **a** maçon **b** mécanicien
c architecte **d** chômeur
e agriculteur

8 **a** ingénieur **b** plombier
c maçon **d** comptable
e gendarme

5 Travel and transport

1 **a** carte **b** aéroport
c avion **d** feux rouges
e circulation **f** bicyclette

2 **a** aéroport **b** gare routière
c station-service **d** aire de
repos **e** transports en commun

3 Gare: composter votre billet
deuxième classe couchette

Aéroport: piste vol AF218
porte No8

Route: essence faire le
plein virage sans plomb

4 **a** ceinture de sécurité **b** autoroute
c consigne **d** direct **e** sortie

5 **a** en provenance de **b** départ
c aller retour **d** monter dans
e décoller

6 **a** circulation **b** réserver
c wagon-lit (OR couchette)
d correspondance/changer
e supplément

7 **a** bateau **b** aéroglisseur
c carte **d** taxi **e** avion

6 Finding the way

1 **a** feux rouges gauche
b deuxième à droite **c** droite
carrefour **d** tout droit pont

2 **a** en face de **b** à côté de
c entre **d** devant

3 **a** derrière **b** avant
c loin d'ici **d** à gauche

7 Holidays, tourism & tourist information

1 **a** payant **b** ouvert **c** après-midi (OR soir) **d** hiver

2 Au bord de la mer: natation
ski nautique planche à voile
plongée sous-marine

En montagne: alpinisme ski
sports d'hiver vacances de neige

Mer ou montagne: excursion

3 **a** nuit **b** après-midi **c** balle
d parc **e** soir

4 **a** pique-nique **b** visite **c** bain
de soleil **d** excursion **e** alpinisme

5 randonnée paysage chaleur
bronzer caméscope côte
séjour nautique groupe
entrée tour

6 **a** all the year round
b pay accompanied (by an adult)
c allowed
d half-hour/30 minutes

8 Accommodation

1 **a** gîte **b** auberge de jeunesse
c camping **d** hôtel

2 **a** lampe de poche **b** poêle
c matelas **d** ouvre-boîte
e sac de couchage

3 Hôtel: chambre de famille demi-pension grand lit

Camping: bloc sanitaire gaz
emplacement sac de couchage

4 alimentation (food shop)
animation (entertainment)
location (hire)
réception (reception)
réservation (reservation)

5 **a** prise (de courant) **b** pièce
d'identité **c** plats cuisinés à
emporter **d** pension complète

6 **a** passeport **b** pièce d'identité
c sale **d** poêle

7 **a** personne **b** location couchage
c chauffée **d** animé
e confirmer écrit

8 **a** descendre faire **b** garer
c rester **d** marche

9 People & places

1 a Pays-Bas   **b** pays de Galles
   c Autriche   **d** Etats-Unis
   e Suisse

2 a les Etats-Unis   **b** Manche
   c l'Afrique   **d** Suisse
   e l'Angleterre

3 a écossaise   **b** américain
   c grecque   **d** belge

4 a Grande-Bretagne   **b** France
   c Italie   **d** Allemagne
   e Etats-Unis   **f** Suède

5 a population   **b** président
   c francophone   **d** nationalité
   e Edimbourg/Ecosse   **f** bilingue

6 Le Royaume-Uni: Irlande du Nord
   Londres   Ecosse

   La France: Normandie   Marseille
   Bretagne   Pyrénées   Midi

   L'Union Européenne: Espagne
   Italie   Autriche   Bruxelles
   Portugal

   Le monde: Afrique

7 a danois   **b** italienne
   c écossais   **d** anglaise
   e espagnol

10 Services (bank, post office, lost property)

1 a iii   **b** v   **c** i   **d** ii   **e** iv

2 a permis de conduire
   b porte-monnaie   **c** batterie
   d formulaire   **e** portable

3 La Banque: chèque   billet de euros
   livre sterling

   La poste: timbre   code postal
   paquet   lettre

   France Télécom: télécarte   indicatif
   portable

4 a timbre   **b** télécarte   **c** volant
   d portable

5 a colis   **b** parapluie
   c montre   **d** paquet
   e chéquier   **f** carte

6 a espèces   **b** crevé   **c** signer
   d numéro   **e** portefeuille

7 a laisser   **b** argent   **c** cuir
   d décrire   **e** perdu

11 Illness, accidents and injuries

1 cou   œil   cheville   bouche
   bras   poignet   estomac   cœur
   corps   nez

2 a pieds   **b** tête   **c** ordonnance
   d comprimé   **e** hôpital

3 sang   pansement   radio
  police   douleur

4 **a** sparadrap   **b** médicament
  c comprimé   **d** sirop   **e** pilule

5 Médecin: rhume   mal de mer
  fièvre   diarrhée   grippe

  Hôpital: jambe cassée

6 **a** rhume des foins
  b piqûre   **c** doigts   **d** plombage
  e mal aux dents

7 **a** front   **b** contrôle
  c cheville   **d** mort

12 House and home

1 **a** grenier   **b** deuxième étage
  c premier étage   **d** rez-de-
  chaussée   **e** cave

2 **a** rideau   **b** échelle   **c** terrasse
  d moquette   **e** fenêtre

3 Cuisine: four   lave-vaisselle
  marmite   cuisinière   congélateur

  Salle de bains: baignoire   douche
  lavabo

  Salon: fauteuil   canapé

4 **a** garage   **b** lave-linge OR machine à
  laver   **c** escalier   **d** cheminée
  e réveil

5 **a** tapis   **b** ouvre-boîte   **c** miroir
  d vestibule   **e** toilettes

6 **a** prête   **b** partage   **c** déménage
  d habite   **e** donne

7 **a** jardin   **b** antenne parabolique
  c évier   **d** clé

13 Life at home

1 **a** se réveiller   se lever   se laver
  se déshabiller   se coucher

  b faire la cuisine   mettre la table
  dîner   débarrasser la table   faire
  la vaisselle

2 laver la voiture   sortir la poubelle
  tondre le gazon   faire du jardinage

3 **a** souvent   **b** de temps en temps
  c toujours   **d** quelquefois
  e tous les jours

4 **a** se réveiller   **b** goûter
  c argent de poche   **d** jardinage

5 **a** me lève   **b** prépare   **c** demande
  d reçois   **e** range

6 **a** poubelle   **b** table   **c** vaisselle
  d lit   **e** gazon

7 **a** l'aspirateur   **b** brosse les dents
  c le repassage   **d** un bain
  e la vaisselle

14 Special occasions

1 **a** la Saint-Valentin   **b** la fête
nationale   **c** le jour de Noël
d la Saint-Sylvestre

2 **a** anniversaire   **b** Noël

3 **a** Bonne année   **b** Bon appétit
c Bon anniversaire   **d** Félicitations
e Bon voyage   **f** Joyeux Noël

4 **a** jour de congé   **b** cadeaux
c feu d'artifice   **d** en chocolat
e carte

5 **a** galette des rois
b noces d'argent
c Santé!
d fête des Mères
e sapin de Noël

6 **a** mairie   **b** chanson   **c** mariée
d félicitations   **e** marié   **f** gâteau
g église   **h** mariage

7 **a** fête   **b** recevoir   **c** envoie
d ouvrir   **e** fait la bise

15 Food & drink

1 Fruit: fraise   poire   citron
pamplemousse

Légume: pomme de terre
petits pois   épinards   chou-fleur

Viande: poulet   agneau   bœuf
saucisson

2 **a** limonade   **b** lait   **c** agneau
d chocolat

3 Potage: poivre   oignon
champignon   pommes de terre
sel

Gâteau: œufs   sucre   cerises
farine   confiture

4 **a** faim   **b** végétarien(ne)   **c** aime
d allergique

5 un œuf   le thon   le lait   le yaourt

6 **a** v   **b** i   **c** iv   **d** iii   **e** ii

7 poisson   pain   huile   oignons
œufs   tomates

16 Eating out

1 **a** restaurant   **b** canard
c dessert   **d** légume   **e** melon

2 **a** iii   **b** i   **c** v   **d** ii   **e** iv

3 **a** hors-d'œuvre   **b** moules
c tarte maison   **d** compris
e service

4 **a** pourboire   **b** apéritif
c mademoiselle   **d** nature
e fruits de mer

5 **a** carte   **b** commander
c pour commencer   **d** monsieur
e plat principal   **f** boisson
g bouteille

6 **a** pizza **b** hamburger
c sandwich **d** crêpe **e** casse-croûte

7 addition bol cuiller assiette verre carafe

17 Healthy living

1 **a** fumez éviter **b** alcool
c crise cardiaque **d** dangereux
e refuser **f** en forme régime

2 **a** santé **b** sport **c** exercice
d équilibré

3 **a** athlète **b** adolescent **c** drogué

4 **a** malheureux **b** inadmissible
c imprudent **d** lent **e** dangereux

18 The world of work

1 **a** collègue **b** scotch
c projecteur **d** réunion
e classeur

2 **a** chanteur **b** employé
c ouvrier **d** paysan **e** coiffeur
f directeur **g** informaticien

3 **a** disquette **b** perforeuse
c fiche **d** clavier **e** logiciel

4 **a** boulot **b** formation
c usine **d** puce **e** colle
f expert consultant

5 **a** vendeur **b** employée
c chirurgien **d** flic **e** coiffeur
f mannequin **g** informaticien
h épicier

6 **a** Allô **b** directeur **c** part
d quittez **e** rappeler

7 **a** disque **b** puce
c formater **d** télécharger

19 Leisure activities

1 **a** arts martiaux **b** échecs
c handball **d** cartes **e** volley

2 flûte violon batterie trompette
piano guitare

3 **a** lecture **b** alpinisme
c voile **d** cyclisme
e promenade

4 **a** fana(tique) **b** sensass
c favori/préféré **d** passionnante
e sportif/sportive

5 **a** patin à roulettes **b** piscine
c bande dessinée **d** passe-temps

6 **a** s'entraîner **b** nager **c** écouter
d lire **e** danser

7 **a** équitation **b** alpinisme OR ski
c match **d** patinoire

20 Media (cinema, television, theatre)

1 Télévision: film d'épouvante
informations chaîne feuilleton

Théâtre: scène pièce balcon
séance

2 **a** vedette **b** lecteur **c** courrier
du cœur **d** image **e** caméra

3 **a** épouvante **b** comiques
   c amour **d** amusantes
   e en noir et blanc

4 **a** émission **b** documentaire
   c publicité **d** série **e** chaîne

5 **a** courrier du cœur **b** jeu télévisé
   c vedette **d** dessin animé
   e presse

6 horreur western épouvante
   comique(s) policier amour
   aventures

7 **a** salle **b** séance **c** écran
   d sous-titre **e** vedette

21 People & personalities

1 Positif: aimable généreux génial
   charmant consciencieux

   Négatif: cruel méchant stupide
   égoïste paresseux

2 **a** héros **b** joueur **c** champion
   d femme **e** peintre **f** homme

3 **a** disputé **b** gagné **c** marqué
   d espère **e** s'entendent
   f fâchent

4 **a** timide **b** intelligent **c** poli
   d de bonne humeur **e** laid

5 **a** bavard **b** sens de l'humour
   c vêtements **d** date de naissance
   e queue de cheval

6 **a** poli **b** sympathique
   c dynamique **d** aimable
   e honnête

7 **a** jaloux **b** pénible
   c cruel **d** égoïste **e** bizarre

22 Meeting people

1 **a** août **b** aujourd'hui **c** soir
   d désolé **e** Au revoir
   f Bienvenue

2 **a** fixer un rendez-vous **b** tutoyer
   c être sur le point de ...
   d aller chercher/venir chercher
   e manquer

3 **a** accepter **b** décidé
   c embrassée **d** proposé
   e remercié

4 **a** à l'heure **b** dans cinq minutes
   c à quelle heure **d** ce matin
   e le lendemain

5 **a** avant-hier **b** hier matin
   c cet après-midi **d** demain soir
   e après-demain

6 **a** certainement **b** à bientôt
   c avec plaisir **d** d'accord
   e ravi **f** merci

7 **a** salut **b** demain **c** bien sûr
   d viendrai te chercher **e** à demain
   f merci

23 Shopping

1 **a** parfumerie **b** faire un paquet-cadeau **c** l'ascenseur **d** kiosque à journaux **e** payé

2 **a** iii **b** v **c** iv **d** i **e** ii

3 **a** supermarché **b** pharmacie **c** librairie **d** épicerie **e** boucherie **f** kiosque **g** marché

4 **a** casserole **b** caméscope **c** jeu de société **d** appareil photo **e** enveloppe

5 **a** bijouterie **b** faire un paquet-cadeau **c** fermeture annuelle **d** douzaine **e** d'une grande valeur

6 **a** réduction **b** pour le prix de deux **c** promotion **d** achetez **e** gratuit

7 **a** affreux **b** réduit **c** fraîche **d** nouveau **e** bon marché

24 Fashion and clothes

1 **a** veste **b** chapeau **c** pardessus **d** maillot de bain **e** chemise de nuit

2 **a** lavage à la main **b** laine **c** nettoyage à sec **d** coton **e** taille

3 vert   gris   rose   blanc
rouge   jaune   brun
violet   bleu

4 **a** costume **b** imper(méable) **c** vêtements **d** fermeture éclair **e** ceinture

5 **a** serré **b** longue **c** rayée **d** court **e** étroit

6 **a** blouson **b** anorak **c** gants **d** manteau **e** écharpe **f** pardessus **g** bottes

25 Current affairs and social issues

1 **a** cambrioleur **b** faim **c** SDF (sans domicile fixe) **d** tiers-monde **e** sécheresse

2 **a** dauphin **b** embouteillage **c** amélioration **d** coup de soleil **e** recycler

3 **a** les pays développés **b** le tabagisme **c** polluer **d** le manque de pluie **e** réfugiés

4 **a** recyclage **b** polluer **c** couche d'ozone **d** environnement **e** ordures

5 **a** avoir tort **b** jeter/détruire/gaspiller **c** occident **d** sécurité **e** pays en voie de développement

6 **a** sans abri **b** drogue **c** tabagisme **d** réfugié

7 a, e, i